# Working With Horses

To Madeleine, John, Charlotte
and Alexander

# Working With Horses

### Alan Smith

DAVID & CHARLES

NEWTON ABBOT    LONDON

NORTH POMFRET (VT) VANCOUVER

ISBN 0 7153 7091
Library of Congress Catalog Card Number 75–29530

© Alan Smith 1975

Set in 11 on 12 point Bembo
and Photoset and printed in Great Britain
by Redwood Burn Limited, Trowbridge & Esher
for David & Charles (Holdings) Limited
South Devon House Newton Abbot Devon

Published in the United States of America
by David & Charles Inc
North Pomfret Vermont 05053 USA

Published in Canada
by Douglas David & Charles Limited
132 Philip Avenue North Vancouver BC

# Contents

# List of Illustrations

# Introduction

The world of horses covers an enormous area, and the work involved with them is almost infinitely varied, be it the thrill of riding a winner on the racecourse or in the show jumping arena; rising long before the dawn on a bitter, frosty morning to get a horse ready to go out hunting; trying to teach a line of young children the first elements of riding; giving a mare all your care, attention and tenderness when she is about to produce her first foal; studying for years so that you can acquire the intricate knowledge that entitles you to look after them as a veterinary surgeon; or learning how to make their shoes and their saddles.

During recent years there has been a great upsurge in interest in horses, and more people are riding purely for pleasure than ever before. Up until only 100 years or so ago, horses were an essential part of the working scene, on farms, or in the cities as a means of transport but, hunting excepted, few people rode them for enjoyment. Then came the internal combustion engine, producing machines which could go faster, farther, pull heavier loads, and the horse as a working animal all but died away. In the last twenty or so years, however, more and more people, adults as well as children, have started to learn to ride, have tasted the enjoyment and excitement, and often enough the feeling of sheer well-being that comes from regular riding. Riding schools, of all shapes and sizes, have mushroomed all over Britain, bringing the opportunity to ride to many who would otherwise never have thought of it. The popularity of show jumping on television, the performances of HRH Princess Anne in horse trials, have given an additional impetus to this widespread interest which has in turn fed upon the extra leisure time that most people have, and which will probably increase even more in the future as working hours grow shorter.

As this happens, as a greater number of young people learn to ride and then develop an interest in all the other facets of stable life, a proportion will want to turn what started as a hobby into a career. It is for such youngsters that this book has been written – for them and their parents and advisers. The 'horsey world' is a strange one; in the first place there are the definite divisions, with the classical dressage riders and the show jumpers, for example, often so far apart in their outlook that one might suppose they were riding entirely different animals; but at the same time there is a good deal of overlapping, and because a person starts work in, say, polo, there is no reason why he or she should not go to a hunting stable and then on to a show jumping yard. Indeed as long as he stays in each one long enough to learn what it is all about, and to repay the work that the head groom or whoever will have put into teaching him, then there is a lot to be said for moving about and learning the job from many different angles.

There are, then, a variety of different jobs, but one thing they all have in common is hard work. If you are thinking of working with horses because it looks a glamorous job with not too much effort involved and a lot of limelight with rich rewards at the end of it, then my only advice is – forget it. Looking after horses, in whatever capacity, is hard work, often in bad weather and frequently uncomfortable conditions – if you and your horse come back soaking wet from a ride you must make sure that the horse is dry and warm before you worry about yourself – and it can be dangerous work too. Moreover if you turn out to be a Lester Piggott you may make a lucrative living out of your work, but the odds are very much greater that you will have to be content with an adequate wage.

What you will get is the chance to work with the horses you love, among people similarly inclined. You will reap the rewards of affection from an animal which depends upon you for its comfort, often for its life. So if you do decide to work with horses you must make sure it is for the right reasons; if it is just the 'glamour' that appeals to you it is far better to do some other sort of work, which will probably earn you more so that you can afford to keep a horse as a hobby. It will be better for the horse and better for you.

If you feel that you really do want to work with them, that you will not be put off and disillusioned by day after day of mucking out, grooming, cleaning tack, all the routine tasks that are the basis of most work with horses, then you still have to decide what sort of work it is going to be. For that you need to look at yourself; weigh up your own character, your advantages and disadvantages, your special likes and dislikes. If, for instance, it is the horses themselves that you like, rather than riding them, you may be best suited to stud work, and if you are physically rather small, then probably at a pony stud rather than a horse one where you may, eventually, be required to handle a highly-strung, powerful thoroughbred stallion. If hunting is your main love, then clearly you should try to work either in a Hunt stable or with someone who hunts regularly, with the possibility that you too will be allowed the occasional day out with hounds. If you ride particularly well and are inclined to be an extrovert, showing horses may prove to be your métier; while if you are not too big, racing may be the answer. This is something you must work out for yourself, and as your whole future could depend upon it, do not try to fool yourself.

There are also a lot of jobs in which, although horses are a vital part, you are not actually working with them. Saddle-making, for example, or in some office jobs in racing, or in bloodstock or travel agencies. These too I have covered, because even if you are not physically working with horses an interest in them, and knowledge of them, is important to the job. Some of the work, for example in bloodstock agencies, is not for people just leaving school or university; some experience is needed even before you can attempt it, and I have tried to show what this experience should be.

It seemed to me as important to stop young people entering into the wrong job as advising how they might find the right one, for it is surely better to have a dream-bubble burst than to waste years, the vital first few years of your working life, going along the wrong road. If this book does either then I shall not have wasted my time.

*Alan Smith*

# Preparation – Examinations and Qualifications

So you have decided that, despite all the snags, you want to work with horses. But where do you start? The worst thing you could possibly do would be to make up your mind that you will leave school as early as you can and look for a job with horses. You would probably find one, as long as you do not mind a lot of hard work and little reward, but after a few years you would very likely be little better off, with hardly any more knowledge, than when you started. You would probably know how to groom and muck out – both, of course, an essential part of the operation – and maybe you would have had a little riding but, unless you were extraordinarily lucky, you would certainly not have learned enough even to be able to take the least of the British Horse Society's examinations, and would have confined yourself to working permanently as a groom and nothing else. Again, well enough if this is what you want, but make sure you do not find yourself travelling slowly along a cul-de-sac when what you really hoped for was the high road to success, with the possibility of riding professionally, or instructing, or perhaps owning or running your own yard.

If you want to make a career with horses, the first essential is a thorough basic training. This begins, as with any other career, at school. The odds are that, if you want to make horses your life's work, you will have been riding while you are still at school, either in the Pony Club or at a local riding school. Well and good, for this will have given you some idea of what is in store, but it should be kept as a holiday, weekend or evening occupation, not impinging on your schoolwork.

There are two main reasons for this. The first is that working with horses, whatever job you finally decide on, is inevitably hard work that can only be done if you are fit and healthy; presumably you are now, or you would not even be thinking of it, but it may not always be so. Even in the best organised of stables, accidents will sometimes happen; illnesses too, which may leave you unable to fulfil the rigorous demands of a life with horses. So what do you do then, if horses are all you know? But if you have a broad general education, perhaps with some specialised knowledge such as shorthand and typing, for example, then you will know that, whatever happens, you can be assured of a decent job.

The other reason is even more immediate, however, and that is the standard of education demanded before a candidate can even sit for a British Horse Society examination.

Let us look, first of all, at the general structure of examinations in the horse world. If you are or have been a member of the Pony Club you will know that there are four tests of efficiency, starting with D, which calls for just the most rudimentary knowledge, and rising to A, which requires a fairly high standard of horsemanship and horsemastership. The Riding Clubs movement also has four similar examinations, while both the Association of British Riding Schools and the National Pony Society award diplomas. All of these, however, are either guides to ability rather than generally recognised qualifications, or else specialised guarantees of a knowledge which applies mainly to one particular sphere of activity.

The qualifications which count most widely, and indeed are recognised and sought after in many countries apart from the United Kingdom, are those of the British Horse Society. The four principal ones are the British Horse Society Assistant Instructor's Certificate, the British Horse Society Intermediate Instructor's Certificate, the British Horse Society Instructor's Certificate and the Fellowship of the British Horse Society.

For those who do not wish to instruct there are the British Horse Society Certificate of Horsemastership – this was called the BHS Horsemaster's Certificate until 1975 when the title was changed as it was felt that it implied too complete a knowledge – and the BHS Stable Manager's Certificate. In addition there are BHS Horse Knowledge and Riding Certificates (in four stages), but these are intended as guides to achievement, primarily for the satisfaction of the persons concerned, and do not carry any special status of qualification although they can be useful to candidates who have taken the BHSAI and are progressing towards the BHSI.

As I have mentioned, academic qualifications are necessary before one can take these examinations, and the standard has become higher. At the beginning of 1974 the BHS Horsemanship and Examination Committee was reconstituted, with one subcommittee set up specifically to review all the society's examinations and tests and recommend changes. The first of these were to the BHSAI, the BHSI and the Certificate of Horsemastership.

Up to October 1976, the minimum academic qualifications needed by a candidate for the BHSAI would be two 'O' Levels or CSE Grade 2 passes. But from that date four 'O' Levels would be required, including English language, English literature or spoken English, and the CSE passes would have to be Grade 1. As the minimum age at which the examination can be sat is seventeen and a half, it is quite clear that your time spent studying at school will by no means be 'wasted'. These academic qualifications do not, incidentally, apply to candidates over twenty years of age.

The other changes made by the new subcommittee were to 'bridge the gap' between the older BHSAI and BHSI with the introduction of the BHS Intermediate Instructor's Certificate and to raise the age at which the BHSI examination could be taken from twenty to twenty-two years, although anyone who had passed the Horse Knowledge and Riding test Grade 4, the Riding Club test Grade 4 or the Pony Club A test could still take it at twenty.

Part of the reasoning behind these changes was the desire to improve the percentage of candidates who passed: in 1973, for example, of the approximately 1,350 people who took the BHSAI examination only about 50 per cent passed, while of the 148 who took the BHSI only 26 passed, and as this is an examination which can be taken in three parts and the 26 included those who passed only their final test, the proportion is even lower.

It was also hoped, and this hope looks as if it may be realised, that by raising the academic qualifications, local education authorities would be more likely to make a grant towards the training that is necessary, instead of dismissing riding as a 'rich man's sport, with no relevance to modern education'.

This might be a good place to deal with the examinations in more detail. The BHSAI examination is in four parts, and the Certificate of Horsemastership covers the first three of them. They are:

1 *Equitation*
Candidates will be examined for their riding in the open and/or in a covered school.
Candidates must have:
(a) A good seat and position and the ability to apply the aids correctly.
(b) A knowledge of the correct basic paces of the horse.

(c) The ability to ride simple school movements (turns, circles, changes of pace and direction, etc).

(d) The ability to jump fences up to 3ft 3in in good style and with fluency, from trot or canter. The course will include doubles and changes of direction.

2 *Stable management and horsemastership*

Candidates must have a sound practical knowledge of how to handle horses and of:

(a) Stable routine – daily programme, ie feeding, watering, bedding, mucking out, sweeping, etc; care and cleanliness of tack room, feed shed, muck heap, etc; care and use of all grooming kit and horse clothing.

(b) Care of stabled horses – feeding, watering, grooming, rugging, exercising; bandaging, recognition of lameness or ill health; preparing horses for a journey, care while travelling; care of hunters and competition horses; reason for clipping, how to clip, types of clip, singeing, plaiting and trimming (manes, tails, heels, etc).

(c) Care of horses at grass – suitability of area, ie terrain, watering, fencing, shelter, poisonous plants, etc; supervision of horses, ie feeding, health, warmth, settling with others, inspection of wounds or sores, protection from flies; how to prepare horses to be turned out or got up from grass.

(d) Saddlery – all types of saddlery in common use, with their respective advantages and disadvantages (saddles, bridles, bits, head collars, boots, etc); fitting, checking and care of saddlery; precautions against injuries (sore backs, galls, etc).

(e) Shoeing – conformation of the foot and care of feet; reasons for shoeing; recognition of well- and badly-shod or neglected feet; reasons for special shoeing; shoeing tools and procedures; how to remove a shoe.

(f) Conformation – basic knowledge of structure of a horse; points of the horse; types and markings.

3 *Minor ailments*

Written paper, normally comprising five questions in forty-five minutes, covering:

(a) Elementary rules of nursing a sick horse; signs of good or ill health; how to take temperature, pulse and respiration.

(b) How to deal with infection and contagion (coughs, colds, flu, strangles, fever, skin diseases, etc).

(c) How to dress wounds, clean cuts, tears, punctures, contusions, galls, sprains, broken knees, etc; how to tub, foment, poultice and hose; knowledge of first aid in an emergency; how to deal with excessive bleeding, shock, colic, azoturia, etc.

(d) How to recognise signs of unsoundness – feet, limbs and wind – and how to diagnose the seat of lameness.

(e) Administration of medicines and the advantages and disadvantages of various methods.

(f) When to call the veterinary surgeon and what information to give.

4 *Instructional ability*

Candidates will be required to give a lesson in the open and/or in a covered school.

Candidates must show:

(a) That they can give a sound lesson on basic equitation.

(b) That they can apply the basic principles of teaching – voice, manner, control, value of demonstration, etc.

(c) That they have the ability to improve their pupils and the knowledge of how to progress to a constructive programme of work.

(d) That they know the principles with regard to safety in the stage management of a ride, lesson or hack.

(e) That they have a knowledge of how to proceed in the case of an accident or emergency to save life or to prevent further injury.

The last question was substituted for the previously-required First Aid Certificate as it was felt that the questions which could be put would be more relevant to working with horses.

Holders of the Certificate of Horsemastership may take section 4 after a period of three months but within three years. They are then entitled to the BHSAI Certificate.

The new BHS Intermediate Instructor's Certificate is in two parts, and only open to holders of the BHSAI.

Candidates must sit the BHS Intermediate Teaching examination. This will test their improved teaching ability. Candidates will be asked to take a ride of four to six pupils, working to improve their positions and control, and also working them over trotting poles and cavaletti. The candidate will also have to show that he or she is capable of preparing candidates up to the BHS Horse Knowledge and Riding test, Grade 3, the Pony Club 'B' test, and of teaching Elementary dressage standard.

The candidates will also be asked to work pupils over show jumps and fixed fences, to the standard of Pony Club or Riding Club Horse Trials. They will then have to give a lunge lesson to a novice adult or child rider. Finally, they will be expected to give a five-minute talk on basic stable management and routine – as though to pupils working for their BHSAI examination.

If successful, this will give candidates the BHS Intermediate Teaching

Working a horse on a lunge-rein is an important part of his education: the rein is kept at full stretch to maintain essential contact

Certificate. To gain the full Intermediate Instructor's Certificate they must also hold either the Pony Club 'A' test, the Riding Club Grade 4 test, or the BHS Horse Knowledge and Riding test, Grade 4.

After 1 October 1976 candidates wishing to sit for the BHSI, or any part of it, must already hold the BHSII.

The BHSI examination is in three parts, which may be taken separately, and each part carries its own certificate. If they are all taken and passed together, a candidate may be awarded BHSI (Advanced). The sections are:

1 *BHS Equitation Certificate*, which is open to holders of the BHSAI, BHS Certificate of Horsemastership, Horse Knowledge and Riding Grade 4, Riding Club Grade 4, and Pony Club A. Candidates must show that they are correct, competent and knowledgeable horsemen with a sound grasp of the principles of training horses, on the flat and over fences.
The syllabus requires work up to and including movements from Medium dressage tests (excluding flying changes), Medium horse trials and Grade C jumping.
Candidates will be required to assess, ride and jump several horses, also to show practical knowledge of training young and spoilt horses – both dismounted and mounted.

2 *BHS Teaching Certificate*, which is open to holders of the BHSAI and to members of the BHS over thirty years of age who can show evidence of some years of instructing experience.

Candidates must show that they are effective instructors with sound teaching and equitation principles.

Candidates will be required to teach to the level of Medium dressage, Novice horse trials and Grade C jumping, and to show their ability to train students and pupils for current examinations and competitions (eg BHSAI, Riding Club and Pony Club tests, dressage, show jumping and combined training).

Candidates will be required to instruct a class and/or an individual mounted and/or dismounted in and/or out of doors.

Candidates are expected to be able to give a short talk as if to students.

3 *BHS Stable Manager's Certificate*, which is open to holders of the BHSAI, BHS Certificate of Horsemastership and Pony Club H test, and BHS members over thirty years old who can show evidence of some years' practical experience assisting in running a yard and caring for a number of horses.

Candidates must show sound, experienced knowledge in all aspects of horse care, eg feeding, exercise, conditioning for various types of work, fitness, health, practical veterinary knowledge, examination for buying and detection and treatment of lameness.

They must also be familiar with all aspects of organising and running a yard, eg staffing, layout, stable contraction, book-keeping, buying fodder and other necessary equipment.

Candidates must be sound in their knowledge of basic principles in the care of mares, foals and youngstock and the management of grassland.

Candidates are expected to be able to give a five-minute talk on a given subject.

Fellowship of the British Horse Society is open to people who, having attained their twenty-fifth birthday and being holders of the BHSI and/or being Fellows of the Institute of the Horse (which was the predecessor of the BHS), produce a testimony or testimonies certifying that they have had two years' practical experience as an instructor during the previous five years.

They will be examined in:

1 Equitation and training the horse
2 Ability as an instructor
3 Ability to take part in a discussion on equitation and training in all their branches.

As there are fewer than twenty Fellows of the BHS practising in Great Britain at present, it will be realised that the standard for this is high indeed; something to be aimed at, although few will achieve it.

Apart from the Fellowship examination and that for Grade 6 of the Horse Knowledge and Riding, which are taken at the National Equestrian Centre at Stoneleigh in Warwickshire, the other examinations are taken at centres throughout the country. Something like 130–140 days of examination are held each year, involving around 1,700 candidates for the BHSAI, BHSI and Horse-mastership Certificates, apart from the Riding Club and Pony Club tests. The chief examiners for the BHS examinations are the practising Fellows and a few of the senior instructors, who are appointed to this task by the BHS.

Supposing you have now left school and wish to study for your BHSAI, how do you go about it? Possibly you have been going to a local riding school, but even if you would like to go on riding there and training for your examinations it is imperative to make sure that the instructors there are capable of giving you that training. The British Horse Society publishes a list of approved riding schools which can be obtained from them; it lists the schools, county by county, with the name and qualifications of the owner or chief instructor, their specialities and facilities, and the examinations for which a pupil will be taught.

There are two ways in which a person may attend a riding school: either as a fee-paying student or as a working pupil. It is probable, and indeed preferable, that either of these courses will be on a residential basis, and should you go as a fee-paying pupil then the course for the BHSAI or the Certificate of Horse-mastership will be about four months. This will be intensive study, including both practical and theoretical work. The alternative, if fee-paying is not possible, is to go as a working pupil, and the majority of schools who prepare students for examination will take a proportion of working pupils.

Clearly if you go on this basis the period of time before you are ready to take your examination will be a good deal longer. The usual arrangement is that a pupil is trained while working for his instruction but will pay for board and lodging, but this may be varied and is a matter for negotiation. No doubt your parents will want to see the riding school, as they would any other school, before sending their child there, and this can often be arranged. It is very important that parents should attend to these matters, and it is also important, although this is a side often neglected, that there should be a specific understanding on the hours each week that a pupil will work, receive training and have time off, and that there should be agreement on the provision of adequate accommodation. The British Horse Society strongly recommends that there should be a written contract, and it is working on the production of a specimen.

The one thing the society does not deal with is the financial arrangements, which must necessarily vary from one place to another according to the work involved, the accommodation and so on; but it does emphasise that the important thing is to receive adequate instruction – that there is no point at all in being a working pupil for, say, three years while training for an instructor's examination and then failing because the training was not good enough, even if, during that time, a student was receiving a little pocket money. He or she might as well have spent the time as an ordinary groom getting a full wage.

Finance is, of course, a problem, and for many years if one could not afford either to go as a fee-paying pupil, or at least live on one's parents while working for instruction, there was virtually no chance of training for a BHS examination. But gradually local education authorities are coming round to the view that this is a training for which they should be prepared to make a grant towards the cost. The increased academic qualifications demanded by the BHS will undoubtedly assist this further.

The government has, by various acts, put the power to allocate grants to school leavers who may wish to study to become riding instructors in the hands of the local education authorities, and so far rather more than thirty of them have shown that they are prepared to do so. Application should be made to the Education Officer of your local authority several months before you intend to leave school; if this request should be turned down, then it is well worth writing to the British Horse Society to ask for assistance. A large part of the time of Colonel Nigel Grove-White, the society's Training and Development Officer, is spent in dealing with matters connected with careers with horses, often general enquiries and also a number of requests for help on matters such as this.

The British Horse Society would then take up the matter with the local education authority concerned and try to make them realise that education in riding is something which is properly conducted and educationally efficient; that an ever-increasing number of people wish to fill their leisure time by learning to ride and that the only safe way to deal with this is by ensuring an equally-increasing number of competent, fully-trained instructors. A number of local authorities have answered that they are not prepared to grant aid for instruction at commercially-run establishments, and of course the vast majority are. But there are now two, and will possibly be more, institutions which run BHSAI courses in conjunction with other studies. These are Newark and Chippenham Technical Colleges, and the courses are residential ones which also include such subjects as secretarial work, which could be very useful indeed if, in time, you come to run your own yard. So if your own local authority is one which refuses to grant aid for you to study at a normal riding school it would be worth applying to either of the above colleges, or getting in touch with the British Horse Society to find out if any other college has started similar courses.

There are other possible sources of financial help, including national family allowances for students undergoing full-time instruction. Claims should be made to the Department of Health and Social Security, Family Allowance Branch, Newcastle-upon-Tyne.

In addition there are various educational charities and foundations which may make small grants to students experiencing special hardship or with special qualifications. The following publications contain information on this:

> *The Annual Charities Register* (which can be referred to at most libraries).
> *Educational Charities* (revised edition, 1962), published by the National Union of Students, 3 Endsleigh Street, London WC1.
> *Trusts and Foundations*, compiled by Guy W. Keeling, edited by Thomas Landau, Bowes and Bowes, 1953.
> *Grants for Higher Education*, compiled by Merle Hastings.
> *Register for Educational Foundations*, compiled by the Legal Department, Department of Education and Science (it can be inspected at that department in Curzon Street, London W1).
> *United Kingdom Post-graduate Awards*, published by the Association of Commonwealth Universities, 36 Cordon Square, London WC1.

A comparatively recent scheme which might also be useful is the Department of Employment's Training Opportunities Scheme. Aid may be granted to someone who has left school for at least three years and then wishes to take further training; the grants are of about £500 and are, at present, for periods of up to four months, but the BHS is trying to have this extended to twelve months which would be of much more value to a working pupil. It is by no means rare for someone who left school and went straight into a stable as a groom to want, several years later, to take the BHS examinations, which would increase his knowledge and job prospects considerably. For such a person the Training Opportunities Scheme, especially if it can be extended, is ideal: application should be made to the local office of the Department of Employment.

An increasing number of local education authorities are running evening classes in riding and horse ownership, but although these may be useful in raising the general standard of knowledge about horses and 'what makes them tick', there is obviously a definite limit to what can be learned in a schoolroom about what is an essentially practical occupation. Such lessons could be of great benefit to parents whose children wish to take up working with horses as a career if they themselves know little of what is involved; it would give them a clearer idea of their child's possible future and also make it much easier to discuss that future either with the child or with his or her instructor.

When the training does start the student would be well advised to find out whether or not he is insured by his employer or trainer in accordance with the Riding Establishments Act, 1970, or the law relating to an employer's legal liability. It may well be that an unpaid student would not be classed as 'employed', and it is most important that he should be covered with regard to accident insurance.

There are, as I have mentioned, other diplomas, which will be covered more fully in the chapters concerning the particular activities they are relevant to. Anyone who has taken and passed the BHS examinations can produce proof that he, or she, is well-trained and qualified and, with the ever-rising increase in interest in riding and the horse generally, should have no difficulty whatever in finding a well-paid, congenial job which he can enjoy while at the same time increasing his equestrian education. For one thing is sure, no matter how many examinations you may take and pass, you will never stop learning as long as you are working with horses.

# Riding Schools

The name of riding school can cover such a wide range of establishments, from the tiniest stable with maybe a couple of ponies teaching children little more than how not to fall off to, say, the world-famous Spanish Riding School in Vienna. Schools are vitally important to anyone wanting to work with horses, firstly as places to learn, and later, for a considerable majority, as places to work in. The 1974 list of riding schools approved by the British Horse Society contained around 300 names, yet it is estimated that in Britain alone the number of schools is about ten times that total. The Association of British Riding Schools also produces a list of approved schools, many of which are also covered by the BHS scheme, but a great number throughout the country are connected with neither. Which is not, of course, to say that they are necessarily any the worse for that, either in the quality of tuition available or of horses and ponies to be ridden, but anyone going to one would have to take it on trust.

The British Horse Society has been running its scheme since 1961, with the objects of:

Providing information as to where, in the opinion of the society, good riding instruction can be obtained.
Assisting in raising the standard of riding instruction and horsemanship through a system of visiting and advising riding schools.

Providing, wherever reasonably possible, adequate third party insurance for approved riding schools for the protection of both client and proprietor.

The society emphasises that the size of the school is immaterial, what counts is the quality, ie sound instruction on well-cared-for horses and ponies, with premises clean and properly run. The schools are inspected before approval is granted, and from time to time afterwards.

The main difference in principle between the approval of the BHS and the ABRS is that the former is done for an independent body and the latter for the committee of the ABRS, but as that committee, naturally, wants to uphold a high standard they are not likely to take a favourable view of anyone, or any riding school, which might lower it. They give a full guide as to what the committee looks for when inspecting a school that has applied for approval:

*General appearance of the establishment*
A tidy yard, and while buildings may be old, they should be warm and dry, and loose boxes should be large enough for horses and ponies to move about easily. Stalls should have partitions high enough to protect animals from reaching each other and biting. Stable animals should have adequate bedding, to enable them to lie down comfortably and to prevent them getting colds and chills from concrete floors.

*Saddleroom*
Saddlery should be soft and supple and in good repair. While it may not be possible to take saddlery to pieces and clean it every day, it is necessary to clean several times a week as this helps to preserve the leather and keep the saddles and bridles in good condition. Special care should be given to stirrup leathers, girths, etc as broken stirrups or girths may result in a serious accident.

*Horses and ponies*
All animals should be in good condition. Animals living out may not look as well groomed as stable animals but coats should still be bright, and when animals come in from a ride and have been sweating, the ears, saddle and girth marks should be rubbed dry. Care of feet will be taken into consideration, also the type of horses and ponies and their age. Approval will not be given to a proprietor who is using two-year-old animals, as they are certainly far too young for riding school work.

*Facilities*
The minimum facilities and equipment are required. There is no grading of schools, therefore large schools who specialise have no priority over a very

small school, and covered schools do not have any preference to an outside manege.

Good grazing is essential if horses and ponies live out, with suitable stabling to tie up the animals for grooming and tacking up. One of the following is necessary – a covered school, an outside manege or some enclosed space for instructional rides. There should be a small number of well-made rustic or painted jumps set up in a paddock or field. Good jumps add to the general appearance of any establishment.

*Instruction*

The standard of the instruction would be assessed on the lesson given, ie Elementary, Intermediate or Advanced. One expects good, sound instruction in whatever grade the instructor is teaching.

The committee of the ABRS make it clear that it does not approve of teenagers under seventeen being in charge of rides on roads, forests or open downland, and would certainly not approve an establishment being run by young people with their parents holding the licence.

One interesting difference is that while the ABRS does not attempt to grade schools, the BHS, in its list, does specify the stage of instruction that a pupil may expect at each of the approved schools. These range from Stage 1, which are described as schools 'doing a good job of introducing pupils to riding at a basic level', to Stage 4, which are fully equipped to take pupils up to the top grades of the Riding Club, Pony Club or Horse Knowledge and Riding tests, with some able to prepare pupils for the BHSI examination.

Riding is a very individualistic sport, and the people connected with it often tend to be antagonistic to anything that smacks of uniformity, so that they spurn examinations or any sort of test. By law all riding schools have to have a licence, which is granted by the local authority, but in many cases that may be the only recognition. Very often people are from backgrounds which have enabled them to ride, probably to hunt, from an early age, so that they have learned their lessons 'the hard way' and see no reason to have to prove it to an examining committee. The snag about this, as far as any youngster setting out is concerned, is that such establishments may be less inclined, or possibly less able, to prepare pupils for the BHS examinations. If, of course, you have already passed your BHSI then there is less of a problem because you will be well equipped to judge whether or not the stable is the sort of place you wish to work at and, if it is, you may well learn a great deal from a really experienced horseman that could never be written into any examination syllabus.

The important thing at the start is to decide what your plans are; they may not, in any case, work out as you wish, but you should have some sort of idea of

Just about all the basic equipment needed for looking after a horse and riding him

what you hope the future holds in store. If you feel that you will be quite happy to be a groom, with no particular ambition to instruct or, eventually, to run a riding school of your own, then clearly the qualifications will not be so demanding. Indeed no written qualifications will be required at all, but what will be necessary are keenness to work hard, because looking after horses is inevitably hard work, and keenness to learn, because the chief instructor or owner of the school will not be happy if he or she has to repeat every little thing that needs to be done every time it needs doing. You will have your daily routine – and routine is important in keeping horses happy as they do not, as a rule, like too much change – and if you can follow this without the constant supervision of instructors who will, themselves, have plenty to occupy their time, you will be that much more appreciated.

The Association of British Riding Schools have a Groom's Diploma which is awarded to any associate or full member of the association who passes what is primarily a practical test of ability. A look at what this examination involves will give a clear idea of what will be expected of you if you do become a groom.

The examination will cover the care of fit, stabled horses, and candidates being competent in all stable duties must show their ability to adapt their knowledge and experience to specialised work, such as hunters, competitive horses, polo ponies, show horses and ponies. Candidates will be required to demonstrate their efficiency in the following:

*Daily routine* – mucking out and bedding down; grooming, clipping, trimming, mane and tail pulling, and plaiting; preparation for a journey; rugging; bandaging.

*Saddlery* – the fitting, care and cleaning of saddlery.

*Shoeing* – recognition of worn or ill-fitting shoes, and ability to remove broken or twisted shoes.

*Feeding* – ability to feed horses in all types of circumstances (ie fit hunters, ponies, etc, and the conditioning and roughing off, and care of sick animals).

*Veterinary* – fomenting, hosing, poulticing, drenching, taking temperature and pulse, dressing and treating wounds.

*Riding* – candidates must show they are practical horsemen, capable of exercising a fit, clipped horse in the open and able to jump small natural fences; be able to ride and lead fit horses and exercise on the lunge; have a knowledge of the Highway Code.

*General* – examiners will take into consideration the candidate's manner in handling horses, also his general approach and tidiness in his work.

*System of marks* – candidates will be given a Pass mark or a Distinction mark.

Explanations will be given to unsuccessful candidates. Examiners will mark to a high standard.

The examination, which starts at 2.30 pm on the first day and concludes at 4.30 pm on the second, is open to candidates aged seventeen and a half or more and who have had a minimum of eighteen months' full-time occupation with horses. The diploma is intended to provide a guide to employers in the selection of competent grooms, capable of working on their own but *not* to be expected to take permanent full responsibility.

The syllabus for the Groom's Diploma will show that, even without the onus of responsibility for the running of the stable or for instruction, there is still a great deal of important work involved if you wish to become proficient at your job but, if you like horses and people, you will find it rewarding. It may be that in very difficult economic times people will have to cut down on the number of horses they keep, no matter what sort of horses they may be — hunters, competition horses or riding school animals — and in proportion the number of grooms needed will be fewer. In which case the better qualified you are, the more you can be relied upon, and the better your chances of good employment.

There is an old saying that 'Those who can do, those who can't teach', but if that is true in the scholastic world it certainly is not in the world of horses. I do not mean that, for example, to train a rider and/or his horse to win Badminton you need to have won Badminton yourself, but almost certainly you will have to have some experience, and some success, in horse trials. Think of the most successful trainers in Britain today, Bertie Hill, Olympic gold medallist in 1956, Lars Sederholm, Alison Oliver, Dick Stillwell, all of them proved themselves in competition before they took to training.

To a large extent, of course, competing in any sort of equestrian activity also involves training — training of young horses and bringing them along to the standard where they can take on, and beat, their rivals. Very few riders consistently perform on 'made' horses for the simple reasons that such horses, if they show any signs of real ability, tend to be expensive, and frequently the riders who have produced them want to keep the horses themselves.

If you are fortunate the riding school that you work in may also have competition horses and you may, when you have gone some way to proving your ability, have the chance to ride them, even if not in competition. Although this could be a very pleasant 'perk' it should not be the main reason for your endeavouring to join such a school, because if riding in competition is your main ambition in life then the odds are that a riding school is not the right place for you. You should try instead for employment in a stable which concentrates on competition, and we will go into these in more detail later.

It cannot be over-emphasised that the choice, out of all the career possi-bilities open to you, of working with horses is only the first stage; there are then the numerous different ways in which you may work with horses. To show you what is involved in each of them is the whole purpose of this book, and it should, one might have thought, have been fairly self-evident that you should pursue the particular activity that most appeals and which you feel is most within your capabilities. Yet a great number of people find themselves in the wrong job, or wrong branch of it, merely because they did not think it out clearly enough or have allowed themselves to be sidetracked. There are some teachers, and not only of riding, who clearly do not like teaching, and they are doing neither themselves nor their pupils any good.

Of course you cannot know when you start your training for a career with horses whether you will like teaching or not, but by the time you have taken your BHSAI you will probably have had sufficient experience to get a good idea. The 'AI' is, naturally, only the beginning of your upward progression, but it should be enough to get you a good job in a riding school where, as well as working, you will still be learning and studying for your Instructor's ex-amination.

Although one finds, all too often, that the only qualification a 'chief instruc-tor' at a riding school has is the BHSAI, the examination was most certainly not intended to show that someone who passed it was qualified for such a re-sponsible position. It might be that, once you have passed your 'AI', you may perhaps even have the chance to run a riding school, but although the respon-sibility may have a lot of appeal it is one that should be resisted. If you want to go on learning it is much better to be a small fish in a big, well-run pond than the master of a puddle that might well dry up.

In an ideal set-up the chief instructor would probably be a Fellow of the British Horse Society or someone of equivalent stature, knowledge and ex-perience, with a number of BHSIs working under him, and a greater number of AIs and those working for their initial examination to complete the staff. In such a school you would clearly be able to see your way up, but even if you cannot find employment at such an establishment it is important to work for someone who knows more than you do, and who can teach you at the same time as you are teaching others.

The teaching of horse and rider is a fascinating subject, and I should think more has been written about it than all the other equestrian subjects put to-gether. It may be true that 'you cannot learn to ride from a book', but you can most certainly learn a great deal if you study the works of some of the 'masters' of the past.

An indoor school is an invaluable aid in the teaching of riders as well as horses: the enclosed space makes it easier for the instructor to control the situation, and lessons can go on regardless of the weather

One of the greatest trainers of recent times was Paul Rodzianko, a Russian cavalryman who came to the International Horse Show in London before World War I and won the King's Cup there, and returned to Britain when he left his homeland after the revolution. Rodzianko had studied under both James Fillis, an Englishman and brilliant rider of Haute Ecole, who went to St Petersburg and was made director of the Cavalry School there, and Federico Caprilli, the Italian whose evolution of the 'forward seat' revolutionised riding, especially over fences, throughout the world. Rodzianko is no longer alive, although a number of his pupils still train, but his book *Modern Horsemanship*, which was published in 1936, still makes fascinating and very informative reading.

Another very useful book, and a much more recent one, is *The Riding Teacher* by Alois Podhajsky, which was published in English translation in 1973. Podhajsky, a former director of the Spanish Riding School in Vienna, was an extremely accomplished rider who could translate his actions into words. The main part of *The Riding Teacher* will be, for the time being at least, way beyond what you will be trying to teach, yet his chapter on 'The Teacher and The Pupil' is relevant right from the beginning of your career. It is too long and detailed a chapter to be summarised here but one sentence is worth quoting in its entirety:

> Three traits of character are an absolute must with any successful riding teacher: he must have self-control, patience and be free of any false ambition.

E. M. Kellock's *The Story of Riding*, published in 1974, although not in itself an instructional book, does illustrate the differences and similarities among a number of the master teachers.

Such reading may seem to you too exalted and high-flown, and of course it is going to be a long time before you are ready, if ever, for the classical High School movements, or for riding round Badminton, let alone teaching others to do so. But there is never any harm in looking at the stars as long as you do not, in the process, get star-struck; and far more important is the realisation that, although it may be many years before you are ready for such accomplishments, if the beginnings are not right you never will be. Teachers of riding, as of any other subject, have a great responsibility – greater indeed than most as it is to both horse and rider. But if you can meet the demands of teaching, it is a most rewarding occupation.

## Trekking Centres

Trekking centres are usually quite different from the ordinary riding school, and there is indeed a considerable variation in opinion as to exactly what a trekking centre's function is. Some such centres will only take people with some experience of riding, and certainly it is preferable that, before setting out on a holiday much of which will be spent on horseback, the people involved should have some idea of what they are about. A great deal of experience is not necessary, because the pace of treks is necessarily slow and therefore suited to riders of limited capability.

Trekking centres mushroomed with the growth of interest in riding after the last war and many of them were far from satisfactory: the ponies were often badly trained – if trained at all – and not well looked after; the people who ran the centres had no idea of tuition, but were content to put untrained riders on untrained ponies and lead them around the countryside. Although the situation is even now not perfect it is a great deal better than it was.

There are two important points to remember if you are thinking of going to work at a trekking centre. The first is that the standard of tuition – if there is any at all – will probably be rudimentary, so that you yourself are unlikely to learn a great deal more than you already know; and the second is that, for the most part, trekking is seasonal work. Meandering across the Devonshire moors or the Scottish highlands on a warm, summer day can be very pleasant, but no one wants to spend a holiday doing so in the cold, wet days of autumn or the snows of winter. So unless the centre is also a riding school most of the staff will be wanted only in the summer, with just a skeleton staff, possibly only the proprietor, to keep things ticking over for the rest of the year.

If, however, you have the time, having perhaps just passed your BHSAI, and the thought of spending a summer leading treks appeals, this can be a pleasant job. Even if you do not learn a great deal more about equitation you will probably encounter some problems with the ponies that you may not have met in your well-ordered riding school. You will also get to know the countryside, because that is what trekking is all about and, most important, you will certainly get to know a great deal more about people. A group of you trekking for perhaps a week will get to know much more about each other than if you spend months going to the same riding school and then going home each day.

Basically treks are divided into day-treks, returning each evening to the same centre, and mounted expeditions in which you set out, probably carrying tents and all the other equipment you may need, to cover quite long cross-country journeys lasting several days over distances of a hundred miles or more.

For young children, or complete novices, the day-trips are the best; they involve carrying no more than, say, luncheon and first aid equipment, and are much less of a strain on both you, as the leader, and those following you. It is important that the size of your party should be kept fairly small – you do not want them straggling way behind you so that you have to keep stopping and taking a roll-call to make sure that no one has fallen by the wayside. It is best if a second-in-command, another responsible member of the centre's staff, can bring up the rear to guard against precisely that, but if this is not possible give the task to the most responsible member of your group and keep aware of what is going on behind you as well as where you are going.

Some parts of the countryside can be dangerous, with boggy ground or steep drops, and it is imperative that you should know the terrain fairly well so that you avoid any unnecessary alarms and accidents.

Mounted expeditions are a much more complex assignment, and involve a great deal of planning beforehand. You must consider the route, the equipment to be carried, and the supply of food for both riders and horses. Ordnance Survey maps of the area are essential, even if it is an area that you have got to know fairly well, because you must always be prepared for the unexpected; tentage and waterproof clothing can often, these days, be very lightweight, which makes it easier for the ponies to carry all that is needed; and food can frequently be bought en route.

Mrs Glenda Spooner, who has done so much to raise the standards of trek-king centres, has written a book *Pony Trekking* which you will find useful, and the Pony Club also publishes a *Guide to Pony Trekking*.

From leading four or five children over the moors to teaching Grand Prix dressage is an enormous step, and will give you some idea of the possibilities open to you if you decide to become a riding instructor. There is one more aspect that deserves, for the immense good it does, to be touched on, and that is riding for the disabled. Although a comparatively new movement, the Riding for the Disabled Association has grown fast throughout the country as doctors, physiotherapists and riding masters have realised just how much benefit chil-dren who are either mentally or physically handicapped, or both, can gain from riding ponies. It gives them a sense of independence which they could get in no other way; it gives them exercise which puts life into muscles they have never used before; it can, and has, turned children who looked likely to be a liability to others all their lives into happy, useful, independent members of the community. There is an increasing number of centres which cater solely, or mainly, for such children, and a lot more do so on a part-time basis.

It may be that you will never become one of the great riding teachers, but if you can help a child to get over his or her disability and live a full, useful life, you will certainly feel like one.

# Competition Horses

## Show Jumping

Probably nothing has done more to stir people's ambitions to work with horses than the success of show jumping over the past twenty years or so. How many people must have acquired a taste for the sport from watching it on television and then going to see it 'live'? It has certainly been a major contributing factor in the considerable increase of interest in riding as a whole. The first time you sit on a pony it is easy enough to daydream and imagine that, one day, you will be beating David Broome or Harvey Smith in a jump-off; the realistic facts – that unless you can afford to own horses of your own, or have the prospect of a wealthy backer, the odds are that you will never even compete against the Broomes and Smiths – have no place in a daydream, unless you are thinking of trying to turn that dream into reality.

Basically there are three ways of working with competition horses: as a groom, as a rider and as a trainer. It is going to be a great many years, even if you have passed your BHSI, before you are likely to be training either horses or riders for competition, except at a fairly low level, so for a start let us look at the first two.

Until 1973 show jumping was, nominally at least, a predominantly amateur sport, but then, following a request from the International Equestrian Federation, whose President, Prince Philip, wanted show jumping to 'put its house in order', the British Show Jumping Association decided that most of the top riders should be made to turn professional. This resulted in considerable changes to the sport, or at least to the general attitude to it. Sponsors came forward with ever-bigger prizes, so that by 1974 prize money in Britain alone had reached over £400,000, of which more than £250,000 came from commercial concerns. Compare this with the first International Horse Show in London after World War II, in 1948, when the biggest prize was £30! The FEI (Fédération Equestre Internationale) decided to bring in professional championships, starting in 1975, and the sport, in Britain especially, has generally taken on an altogether different flavour.

More and more indoor schools have been built, and shows are put on throughout the winter, so that show jumping, which had for so long been purely a summer sport, has become an all-the-year-round one. And this, of course, has had a considerable effect on those working in it. But let us start at the beginning.

Although no qualifications may be needed if you want to work as a groom in a show jumping stable, clearly the more you know, and can show that you know, the more likely you are to find a place in a successful yard. So it would certainly be worth your while taking the BHS Certificate of Horsemastership – which is the BHSAI without the Instructor's section. The work of a groom, no matter what sort of horse you are dealing with, involves a good deal of routine work; mucking out and bedding down, grooming, feeding and watering, tack cleaning and, if you are working for a methodical stable master, keeping everything neat and tidy – these are the things that you will be expected to do in any grooming job.

But working with show jumpers also entails a good deal else. For a start you are dealing with often very expensive animals; not as expensive as racehorses perhaps, but nevertheless horses which, even if they are just promising youngsters, may have cost something running into five figures, and if your charge is a top-class international jumper he might well be worth £25–30,000 or more. To a certain extent horses take very much the same looking after no matter how much they may be worth – the old racing saying that 'A bad horse eats as much as a good one' applies equally to the amount of work involved – but whereas if a novice is out of action for two or three weeks because of a minor mishap there is no particular harm done, if a top Grade A horse is unable to jump for a few weeks during the height of the season, it could well cost several thousand pounds in lost prize money. To take an example, Fred Hartill's great horse Pennwood Forge Mill, on whom Paddy McMahon won the European Championship in 1973, was one of Britain's selected challengers for the World Championship at Hickstead the following year. The world title is fought over

Sally Warren and Pennwood Forge Mill. Sally was the horse's groom for several seasons, including 1973 when Paddy McMahon and Forge Mill won the European championship

three qualifying rounds, with the top four going into the final; and after the first two rounds Pennwood Forge Mill – for whom Mr Hartill had, the previous summer, turned down an offer of £100,000 – looked sure to be one of the four finalists.

But somewhere, at sometime, the horse had damaged a neck muscle, and in the third and final qualifier he just could not give his best; they dropped right out of the running, which cost Paddy his chance of being the first professional rider to win the world title – as he had been the first professional to take the European – and Forge Mill had to be laid up for several weeks while he had treatment; weeks during which such valuable shows as the Royal International, Dublin and the £18,000 Benson & Hedges Pro-Am International were run.

This particular accident happened while the horse was jumping and there was nothing that Sally Warren, at that time Forge Mill's devoted groom, could have done to prevent it. But it shows the financial loss that can be incurred when a top-class horse is out of action, and quite often minor ailments can be prevented from becoming serious if they are spotted in time, and an attentive groom should be ever on the alert.

The one thing that a show jumping groom can be sure of is travel. From the time the outdoor season starts in Britain – in March or early April – until September, the show jumping horses are taken from one show to another: to Hickstead, to the county shows all around the country, to London for the Royal International, often away from home for weeks at a time. The show jumping circuit has often been described as a circus, and in many ways it is – a fleet of caravans and horseboxes packing up as soon as one show is over and moving on to the next. If you like to stay in one place show jumping is not for you, but if you like to get around and are prepared to rough it a bit, often sleeping in the horsebox, then there is plenty of variety and excitement to be had.

Travelling can be as exhausting for horses as jumping, so you will have the additional responsibility of caring for them then, preparing them for the journeys and making life as easy as possible. And making sure, too, that all the equipment you and the rider and horse will need is loaded; it is not so long ago that a well-known rider, having methodically ensured that everything he and his horse might need had been put into the horsebox by the groom, drove to the show, lowered the ramp and discovered that everything he needed was there – except the horse! An extreme case, of course, but a reminder to check everything.

If you work for an international rider your travels will take you very much farther afield: almost every year Britain sends teams all over the Continent; to Rome, Germany, France, sometimes to Spain and Portugal or even behind the

Iron Curtain to the Polish International show at Olsztyn. Periodically teams also go on the North American circuit; to Washington, New York and Toronto. Then, of course, there are the biggest competitions of all – the Olympic Games. The chance of getting to these is a slim one, but when you are experienced as a groom with show jumpers your chances of travel are not limited merely to working for British riders; good grooms from this country are in demand all over the world.

The British Horse Society receives hundreds of letters from many parts of the globe from people who want to employ British grooms; they have to reply that they cannot themselves arrange this, not only because, if they did, it would become a full-time job for staff they can ill-afford to spare, but because they could not be responsible for the abilities and conscientiousness of the groom, nor of the would-be employer. And here a word of warning. The BHS advise such enquirers to advertise, either in national newspapers or such magazines as *Horse and Hound, Riding* and *Light Horse*, but if you see an advertisement that tempts you make sure that you get the fullest possible details about the work involved and the sort of establishment you would be working for. You do not want to travel hundreds, maybe thousands, of miles to discover, the moment you arrive, that it is not at all what you had been expecting.

There is no limit to how far you can go, as Chris Larter discovered and wrote about in her book *Around the World – For a Horse*. Chris, born in Yorkshire and horse-mad from an early age, describes very vividly what it is like to work as a groom in a show jumping stable in this country. During this time she met up with the New Zealand Olympic horse Saba Sam, and eventually finished up – still looking after the horse – back in New Zealand. And you cannot go much farther than round the world.

It may be that your ambitions extend beyond grooming show jumpers and that you will hope to ride them. Your chances of doing so will depend a good deal on the sort of stable you are in; if it is a big one with a lot of young horses, then clearly there is a better chance. No matter how energetic a rider may be there is obviously a limit to the number of horses he can ride, and in any case during a lot of the summer he will be away riding at shows. Maybe you will be too, but perhaps you will be given the chance to bring the youngsters along at home, quietly getting them towards the stage when they can be prepared for competition themselves. Whether you get this chance, and what you do with it, will depend on a lot of things: luck will be one of them, but more important are ability and persistence. By ability I do not mean riding ability alone, but also the capacity to 'think out' a competition, to plan the sort of round you are going to ride to your best advantage. There are a number of quite excellent riders who are just not good competitors because they lack this particular flair.

However, even if you do not 'make it' as a competitor, if you are a good schooling rider you will much increase your own market value, and the best way, indeed the only way, is practice. Someone like Fred Hartill, always looking for another Pennwood Forge Mill, has literally hundreds of horses and ponies passing through his yard each year, selling on most of them quickly, keeping a few to try a little more fully, weeding these down to the minute proportion who might, just might, become potential international horses and then trying them out in competition. In such a situation clearly more than one rider is needed, and it was this that, with Paddy McMahon kept busy on the international circuit and the top home shows, Donna Smith, New Zealand-born but now married to one of Fred Hartill's staff, earned her chance. Riding the youngsters at home she had shown her sympathy with them; she was eventually given the chance to ride in the ring as well, and a good job she made of it.

Harvey Smith and Trevor Banks, who went into partnership in 1973, work on an even bigger international scale, and at the valuable Courvoisier Cognac Championships which followed the Horse of the Year Show at Wembley in

Rodney Jenkins and Idle Dice, winners of more prize money than any other show jumpers in the world: Jenkins was the first professional rider to be chosen for the United States official international team

1974 Harvey, Paul Darragh – the young Irishman who left his own country to join their yard in Yorkshire – and Willie Halliday – a protégé of Harvey's who left, went to Canada and then returned – were all needed to cope with the huge string they had jumping there – sometimes all three of them jumping in the same competition.

There are only a limited number of big, professionally-run yards such as these and in most cases the dealing side is as important financially as the jumping. So that even if you do not ride in competitions, if you can 'make' or improve youngsters, and in so doing increase their value, you will be very much in demand.

## Showing

Showing is a very different matter and, as far as prize money is concerned, very much the poorer, although your chances of riding in the ring are probably higher, assuming you have the ability. Almost every show, of the hundreds throughout the season, has its show classes for hunters, hacks, cobs, Arabs and part-bred Arabs, ponies and – an increasing interest in recent years – driving classes.

Ponies will be dealt with separately, but among the others there is a tremendous choice. Hunters are the biggest section of show horses and they, as you probably know, are divided into Ridden and Led classes. The led hunters – broodmares or youngstock from foals up to three-year-olds – are very often exhibited by the people who bred them, and if you go to work at a stud – work which is covered in another chapter – you may well find yourself in the show ring purely incidentally. Arabs and ponies also have Led as well as Ridden classes, but the others are shown entirely under saddle or, in the case of driving classes, hackneys and the like, in harness.

With any show horse the preparation is quite different from what is required for a jumper, but among the various types of show horse there is also considerable variation, and men who can produce show hunters and show hacks equally well and successfully are rare indeed. So the first thing you have to decide is what sort of show horse you want to be associated with; of course you may decide one thing and then, after a while, change your mind. There is no harm in this, quite the reverse in fact as you will be gathering experience and knowledge as you go along, but do not change too often or too rapidly; no one will be keen to employ a groom who has a reputation for staying only a few weeks.

There are some men, people like Jack Gittins and Roy Trigg, who year after year produce good show hunters, or even if the animals of a particular vintage are not very good, they have the ability to make them appear perhaps a little better than they are or would seem to be in less capable, less experienced hands. And appearance is all-important because in show classes what matters is what the judge thinks of your horse.

If you can work, for a while at least, with one of the acknowledged masters of the showing world you will learn a great deal, but if you are receptive and observant enough you can learn a lot merely from watching them at shows. Show hunters should be bold, able to gallop – although only in working hunter classes will they be called on to jump – and their conformation must be good, although they will be more 'onward bound' and less elegant and tittupping than a show hack. A show horse will not be as hard in condition as a show jumper but it must look really fit and well.

If this sort of work appeals to you, you may well find yourself in a small stable, working for the two- or three-horse owner who hunts and likes to show a bit as well, or perhaps has an old mare from whom he breeds and wants to show off the youngstock. Although I have tended to divide up the various sorts of grooming job this has been principally to make it easier to show the sort of work involved; of course there can be a lot of overlapping and if you love horses you will enjoy this and seize the chance to learn as much as possible. If you work at a riding school, for example, there may well be some horses at livery there which the owners want to be shown, and this could give you your chance.

Although the British Horse Society examination and qualifications can stand you in good stead when it comes to getting a job, they are no more than stepping stones, or mounting blocks if you like, to help you get started, and the rest is up to you. Showing horses well is a mixture of a lot of things; good horsemanship naturally, a constant study of what particular judges like or do not like, a certain amount of gamesmanship, a lot of very hard work combined with a refusal to be downhearted when things go wrong and the duck you thought was a swan is put at the bottom of the line – you will learn soon enough that it is no use to fool yourself about the merits of a horse – and a flair for showmanship. But probably the most important of all these is hard work.

## Horse Trials

No equestrian sport has grown so quickly in recent years as horse trials, despite the confusion that still reigns over what its title should be – the committee that runs it in Britain is the Combined Training Committee, the trials are sometimes called three-day events (although these nowadays usually last for four days), on much of the Continent it is known as the 'Military', because its origin was as a test for officers' chargers, and in France it is known as the Concours Complet – the complete test – which most aptly describes the sport. Britain's success internationally – Olympic gold medals in Mexico and Munich, world and European titles – and the participation of HRH Princess Anne – European Champion in 1971 – with all the publicity attendant upon that, have all helped to make this a sport which is bursting at the seams, so that the increasing number of one-day horse trials each season are mostly filled to capacity with entries, and not a few have to turn some away.

International success and publicity may be part of the reason, but another very important aspect is that it is possible for people to take part, and sometimes win, with horses which do not necessarily cost a fortune. To win a race a horse needs a lot of speed; to win a major show jumping competition these days it must have great power; to be a great dressage horse it must have tremendous presence and action and be able to stand up to years of intensive training. An event horse must have a bit of all these things, but does not have to be a super-horse: it may be one of course, like Cornishman V which Mary Gordon-Watson rode to win a world and a European championship and an Olympic team gold medal – Richard Meade having also won one on him four years earlier – and then the horse will be a world-beater, but reasonable scope, good sound training and skilled riding can get a lesser horse a long way up the horse trials ladder.

This is why the vast majority of trials horses belong to the one- or two-horse owner, and if you decide you want to work in this field you may well find you and the owner – or maybe only you – will be doing all the work. This is not necessarily a bad thing, because it also means that you will be going to most of the trials, possibly getting a lot of riding if the owner works and may quite likely be given the chance to ride in competitions yourself. You may have the satisfaction of bringing a young horse along from scratch, through the novice and intermediate stages of the one-day trials, to taking part in, and perhaps even winning, the classic three-day events – Badminton or Burghley.

Although a groom looking after trials horses will not travel as much as one caring for show jumpers he, or she, will still get around the country a great deal with the possibility of occasional trips overseas. In the early stages an owner will probably keep his horse or horses to trials as local as possible, to save on expenses, but as they progress so they will travel farther afield, from Devonshire to central Scotland, in search of experience and success. In schooling a horse for dressage, to go across country and to show jump, a rider is himself learning all-round horsemanship that must be useful even if he should eventually decide to branch out into a different sort of equestrian endeavour, and so it seems logical to suggest that this is the ideal way to start.

Steve Hambidge, who works for Janet Hodgson, did not start in a trials stable but moved there some years ago after meeting Janet several times while out hunting, talking to her about the sport and deciding he liked the sound of it. Janet, of course, is right at the top of the horse trials ladder: winner of Burghley in 1972, third at Badminton in 1974 and fourth in the world championship the same year. All these achievements were on Larkspur, bought 'for a song' by Janet's father, who has a good eye for a horse, so there are always a number of novices and Steve is given one of his own to train and ride in competitions.

Because the majority of trials-horse owners ride the horses themselves, there is not a great deal of opportunity to be paid to ride – unlike show jumping it is still very much an amateur sport though inevitably getting less so as it grows in popularity – but for those who can make the grade there is the possibility of becoming a trainer of competition horses and riders. Exceptional ability is needed, but for those who have it the opportunities are there.

One of the most unlikely success stories in this sphere has been that of Swedish-born Lars Sederholm, who came to Britain to work as a groom for the noted dressage rider and trainer Mrs Joan Gold and is now himself one of the most successful trainers in the country. Lars's family was completely non-horsey, and he was thirteen before he started riding in earnest. A period in the Swedish Cavalry Cadet Training Unit and two years with the dual Olympic dressage gold medal winner, Henri St Cyr, gave him a good grounding, however, and when he came to Britain he soon made his mark, both training and riding, and was the leading horse trials rider for three years in succession in the early 1960s. Now the training establishment which he and his wife Diana run at Waterstock, near Oxford, is one of the most famous in the country.

For three years while Lars was with Mrs Gold, Alison Coulter, now Alison Oliver, was also there, having already ridden in a number of horse trials and three-day events, and the two of them both freely acknowledge the help that each has given the other. Alison is now another of the country's top trainers, with Princess Anne among her star pupils.

One of the most successful of all the riders-turned-trainers was Bertie Hill, who won many point-to-points, mostly in his native Westcountry, and then turned also to horse trials when the sport began its rise to popularity in the early 1950s. So well did he take to it that he finished seventh in the 1952 Olympic Games and then was a member of the gold medal team in Stockholm four years later, riding Her Majesty the Queen's Countryman III, who he had owned and trained before the horse was bought by the Queen. Bertie, who was the leading point-to-point rider in 1964, had a bad fall the following year and decided to concentrate on training. In 1967 he was asked to train the team for the European championships and the following year for the Mexico Olympics, and in both the team was successful, ending a long period 'in the wilderness' and beginning a run which went unbeaten in major championships through the next Olympics, including a world and two more European championships, until 1973. After Mexico the selection committee decided against having a team trainer, but Bertie has trained a number of individual horses and riders who have been successful, including Janet Hodgson and Mark Phillips.

Dick Stillwell's top performances in the saddle were in show jumping competitions, particularly on High Court who won the Daily Telegraph Cup at the Horse of the Year Show two years running, and he still jumps occasionally, but his training has been equally beneficial to both show jumping and event riders. Dick has the knack, in a short while and few words, of being able to pick out faults and correct them; Mary Gordon-Watson, Richard Meade and Derek Allhusen are among the many that he has helped along the road to victory, and a few years ago he had the interesting and unusual job of training the Greek team for the Balkan Games.

There are a number of other examples – Sheila Willcox, for instance, who was the most successful woman horse trials rider ever and one of only two people to have won Badminton three times. She had to give up riding in trials after a disastrous fall at Tidworth, and although advised not to ride at all she came back to take part in dressage events and mainly to train. In late 1974 she was asked to train the Canadian team for the 1976 Olympic Games in Montreal.

Not all trainers have been so successful in competition of course, but most of them have done reasonably well, and at least had sufficient experience to be able to refer to practical as well as theoretical matters. Not only is competitive experience useful in itself, but it will give you a confidence which is absolutely essential in the training of both horse and rider. This is not to say that you will always be right, to the contrary, and if you are sufficiently sure of what you are doing you will be able to admit this, but nothing is more bemusing to a green horse or a novice rider than half-hearted instruction, given as though you are not sure yourself whether it will work or not.

All this, naturally, is years ahead, but it is some indication of what can be achieved with hard work, thorough training and a receptive frame of mind, so that you never feel that you 'know it all' but will look for ways to improve your own knowledge to the benefit of your pupils.

# Hunting

With the exception of racing, hunting is a bigger employer than any other equestrian activity, and highly-satisfying work it can be. But hard, make no mistake about it, especially during the season; early rising, duties often not finished until late at night, and a great deal to occupy you during the time in between. But as a reward you will be closely involved with one of the oldest of sports, which has become an integral part of life in the British countryside over the past 300 years. It is generally agreed that the second Duke of Buckinghamshire, who died in 1688, was the first Master of a regular pack of foxhounds in Great Britain. The ramifications that have grown out of it since are enormously varied: a tremendous volume of literature, fiction and fact; some of the best of sporting art; a huge horse-breeding industry, aimed at producing the ideal horse to ride across country; National Hunt racing; and so on.

Work in hunting can be split into several divisions, the first being the difference between working in Hunt service, that is to say on the staff of a pack of hounds, and working with hunters, which is principally work as a groom with a reasonable amount of riding exercise, sometimes perhaps as second-horseman, and possibly also having a day out with hounds as a 'perk'.

In Hunt service there are two main divisions, riding and non-riding, with the kennel-huntsman in overall charge and answerable to the Master; under him on the riding side are the whippers-in, second-horsemen and grooms; and in the kennels are a kennelman and under-kennelmen, and also the earth-stopper/terrier-man, who plays such an important part in the successful running of a day's hunting. How many there will be in each of the categories will depend upon the number of horses and hounds kept, which in turn is governed by the number of days on which the country is hunted.

Mr Jorrocks, Surtees's famous fictional hunting enthusiast, described the requirements of a huntsman as needing to be 'strong, active, bold and enterprising . . . he must be desperately fond of hunting, and indefatigable in the pursuit of it. He must be shrewd, sensible, good-tempered and sober; exact, civil and cleanly; a good horseman and a good groom; his voice must be strong, clear and musical; and his eye so quick as to perceive which of his hounds carries the scent when all are running, and he must have so excellent an ear as to distinguish the foremost hounds when he does not see them. He must be quiet, patient and without an atom of conceit.'

The conditions of hunting these days have changed considerably since the times of Surtees, not often, it must be admitted, for the better, but if any man could match up to this ideal he would undoubtedly be as sought-after now as then. At least it gives something to aim at, and a list of the sort of qualities needed if you hope, as presumably you will if you are contemplating hunting as a career, one day to be a professional huntsman.

Certainly a would-be huntsman must be indefatigable, for this is a full-time job to such an extent that it excludes almost all other interests. Many people who go out hunting, even those who do so regularly and should know better, seem to think that a huntsman's duties start at the meet and end when they all go home; in fact the actual business of hunting the hounds is only a part of all he does, the climax and the reason for it all, but nevertheless only the visible peak of the iceberg. No matter how good a huntsman may be in the field, the success of his pack of hounds will have its foundations at home in the kennels.

A huntsman dedicated to his task will be equally dedicated to his hounds; to the breeding of them, the whelping, training of the young entry, selection and then getting them fit for the next season's hunting. He will know his hounds intimately and they him, or how else will he be able to control them in the field. For a huntsman the horses are secondary to the hounds, but naturally they too are his concern; buying the best sort of horses possible for the type of country – and with the money available – seeing them well-cared for and made fit and ready for the season.

The foxhunting season starts officially on 1 November, but before that is cubhunting, so the horses will need to be brought up from grass – assuming they have been turned out – in August for their fitness training. Hounds, too, will be walked out in the summer, with whoever is accompanying them – and

A meet of the Grafton Foxhounds. Bringing hounds to a meet and looking after them in the field is but a part of the Hunt servant's work, much of which goes on out of public view in the stables and kennels

this, too, will be the huntsman whenever possible – either walking or possibly on a bicycle, which is a good way to get a man fit as well.

In the field a huntsman must obviously be good at his job but he will have to be something of a diplomat as well; civility was always necessary but these days, with more people going out hunting who are not too conversant with what is going on and therefore might well do something to spoil the day's sport or at least impede it, with the growing clamour of the anti's – which is not to say that their numbers are necessarily increasing – and most important of all with the need to avoid antagonising the 'fringe' area – which is probably the largest of all – who are neither particularly for nor against hunting, every huntsman, indeed everyone who goes out hunting is, to use a cliché, an ambassador of the sport who must defend it against those who would like to see it abolished.

Peter Beckford, one of the most knowledgeable of the hundreds of men who have written about hunting, once asserted that a good whipper-in was more important than a good huntsman. Not many would agree with him on that, but it is an indication of how important the job is. Ideally there would be a first and a second whipper-in, but more often than not nowadays one man has to suffice for the tasks of both. His job is to act, in the field, as the huntsman's right-hand-man; to complement him in the control of hounds without ever trying to usurp the huntsman's position of authority; to be aware of all that is going on around and to try to prevent it interfering with the business of hunting foxes, while the huntsman is concentrating on his hounds. If there is a second whipper-in he will be responsible for ensuring that no hounds get left behind when a pack is moved on from one covert to another, and if a group of them should go off then he must recover them no matter how long it takes.

In addition a whipper-in is expected to take his full share of the many tasks in the kennels, and some would regard these duties as equally important if not more so; the Lonsdale Library book on foxhunting, published in 1930 but with a lot that is still relevant, says of whippers-in: 'Although their vocal or equestrian powers in the field may not be of the highest order, if the whippers-in perform their duties in the kennel with care and energy, much will be forgiven them.' Like the huntsman, a conscientious whipper-in will spend as much time as possible with hounds, but he will need to do a lot of the menial jobs that working with any animals involves, keeping both the animals and their habitation – be it kennels, stables or whatever – as clean and sanitary as possible.

The position as second-horseman is the first rung in the ladder from groom to whipper-in, and is not so much a substitute for grooming duties as an addition. As its title implies, it involves taking out a second horse for the Master, huntsman or whipper-in on to which they can change as and when the need arises. Because whoever it is will not exactly relish changing from one tired horse on to another, it is imperative that the second-horseman should give his charge as little exercise as possible while getting to wherever the change-over is to take place.

Working as a Hunt servant starts, on the riding side, as a groom; and this can be hard work, with especially early rises during the cubhunting season, when the meets may be at 6.30 am and work in the stables starts a couple of hours before that. First the horses that are going out hunting will need to be prepared, and when they have gone the other horses will have to be exercised and all the normal stable routine gone through. It may well be getting dark by the time the horses return, but still they have to be looked after, and if a groom has two to do it will be getting on for bedtime before they are finished. But at least for those not themselves out hunting there will be the probability of an hour or two off during the middle of the day, and with modern transport to get hounds, horses and riders to and from a meet the day is not as long as it used to be.

In his book *Huntsmen of Our Time* Kenneth Ligertwood wrote a series of pen-pictures of some of the foremost exponents of the art of hunting foxes, including George Gillson, who started in Hunt service before World War II and recalled how he, while a second-horseman with the Essex Staghounds, had had to take horses by train leaving at 6 am, finish the day's hunting at 5 pm and then start the forty-three-mile journey back, arriving home at two o'clock in the morning. After which he was still expected to be up and ready for work again at six o'clock.

A groom in a hunting stable is in a similar situation to one in a racing stable in as much as, having his – or more likely her – two to do, he will be very much responsible for their well-being. Although there may well be a stud groom in overall charge of the stables – the equivalent of a head lad – when the horse comes home, tired probably after a long hard day, with an odd cut or knock maybe, he will hardly be able to give them all an immediate and thorough inspection. So from the groom a cursory brush-down just will not be enough; the horse must be thoroughly looked at and looked after, any minor injuries attended to and any major ones, or anything that looks as if it might develop into something major, reported at once. By the end of a long, hard season a Hunt stable is likely to have far more lame horses than it wants, sometimes more lame than sound ones, and anything you can do to alleviate this situation will be much appreciated.

Although weight is clearly not as important as it is in racing, still anyone contemplating a career in Hunt service should not be too heavy; a riding weight of around 11st 7lb would be about right. It is naturally important to be able to ride, and although an inability in this direction would not necessarily debar anyone from being employed on a Hunt staff, naturally some experience and talent in the saddle is a considerable advantage. As in all jobs, the more experience the better, and if you have been out hunting so much to the good; most Pony Club branches are associated with their local Hunts, so this should not be too difficult to arrange. It is an indication that equestrian ability among Hunt staff is not all that it might be that the Master of Foxhounds Association (the MFHA), in conjunction with the British Horse Society, is planning to run a course or courses to help improve their riding. It is all very well for members of the field to have some difficulty in this respect, but for a member of the Hunt staff riding must be something akin to second nature or it will distract his attention from the job in hand.

Although work in Hunt service is hard, with long hours mostly out-of-doors and frequently in the worst of the weather, there are more girls doing the work than men. One needs to be reasonably strong, for a big, fully-fit hunter can be quite a handful, but girls, with their tact and diplomacy, often with better hands, can be as or more effective than men who often try to rely on sheer strength. There is no reason why a girl should not make a successful career in Hunt service; there are probably more girls riding second horse now than men, there are lady whippers-in and at least one lady huntsman.

Because of the often irregular hours that are worked and because grooms are quite often accommodated in situations where they have to feed themselves, it is all too easy to slip into a habit of living on snacks, bars of chocolate and the like, but it is essential to eat properly; just as important as that the horses and hounds are properly fed, and you would hardly think of neglecting that. It is possible to get 'promotion' to the riding side of Hunt service from working in the kennels, but this is less likely: working in the kennels can, of course, be a perfectly satisfying job in its own right, but as this book is to do with working with horses suffice it to say that quite often the jobs overlap and the important thing is to remember that you are part of a team without a strict line of demarcation.

If the idea of Hunt service appeals, as well as learning to ride, it would be worth your while following your local hounds as much as possible, either on foot or with the aid of a bicycle. You will learn a lot from the other followers and from the Hunt staff too, when they see that you are keen. And as soon as possible you should learn to drive, for this, though apparently incidental, will become gradually more important as you have more responsibility for getting horses, hounds and yourself to a meet.

Hunting is no more a path to easy riches than any other equestrian activity, and less than some; wages are, roughly, in line with the agricultural wage, and accommodation is usually found or provided, because Hunt servants must obviously be near their work. There are certain 'perks' and Christmas Boxes, and there is a Hunt Servants Benefit Society which, if joined, ensures that a member is looked after in case of sickness or accident; and most Hunt servants are able to enjoy a comfortable retirement.

As well as in Hunt service, hunting provides an enormous number of jobs connected with the horses of those who go hunting. Mostly these are grooms jobs and are basically similar to the work of a groom in Hunt service; the starting hours may not be so early, but they are necessarily still early enough to deter those who prefer to stay abed in the morning, at least until the light of dawn. Very often the job will be private, with a family who have just a few horses, possibly just two or three, and you may be the only person working there.

This sort of employment will depend for its success on a number of factors, principally the sort of people you are working for. They may welcome you as almost one of the family, or they may treat you as someone there to do a specific job of work which you are expected to get on with, either of which can be well enough if it accords with your own personality. But all too often the title 'girl groom' is found to cover a multitude of other chores: helping in the garden, or in the house, or with the children to the extent that you are practically a nanny as well. It may, again, be all right with you to do things that have no connection with horses, but it is important to make sure, before you take the job, exactly what your duties will consist of. Then there will be no feeling of being 'put upon'.

There can be advantages about working in private establishments. If the owner is a keen hunting man he will probably have a number of horses, so that not only will you have a lot of practice and riding exercise, but quite possibly you will also be allowed, or even required, to go out hunting yourself; perhaps on a young horse or on one belonging to a child away at school. If you are working alone, or are one of two or three, being able to drive will probably be essential, as well as being to your own benefit.

Although there are no particular examinations for a hunter groom, anyone who has passed the BHSAI would clearly be welcomed as having the sort of knowledge which would stand him in good stead in any of the minor emergencies that may from time to time occur in a stable. There are all sorts of other activities connected with hunting in which you may get involved: hunter trials and point-to-point racing in particular, as well, possibly, as horse trials, for most of the graduates of that sport have originated in the hunting field. Quite possibly you will not only be able to help in these pursuits but may be given the chance to ride in them as well.

Working as a hunter groom, as opposed to being in Hunt service, is a seasonable occupation, and it may well be that you will need to find something to occupy yourself during the summer. Though do not forget that after a hard season, you, like the animals you have been looking after, will be all the better for a holiday. Show jumping or showing might once have been thought ideally complementary activities but, especially with the former, the season is now so long that the two overlap by probably too big a margin to be quite practical.

Trekking, which is essentially a summer occupation, might well fill the bill, and the slower pace could perhaps be a pleasant relaxation before the hectic activity of the winter months. Or again it may be that the stable you are working at also has jumpers or event horses, in which case the problem of summer work does not arise.

For a groom with some experience and who is prepared to work hard, finding employment as a hunting groom is not difficult: at the right time of the year the specialist magazines, *Horse and Hound, Riding* or *Light Horse* for example, are full of 'situations vacant'. There is also a Hunt Servants and Grooms Registry, run by the Masters of Foxhounds Association, details of which can be obtained from the MFHA Secretary, Lieutenant Colonel J. B. S. Chamberlayne, The Elm, Chipping Norton, Oxfordshire.

There is, perhaps, no harm in repeating that this is by its very nature hard work with long hours, but it gives the chance of being paid to do something which many people give a great deal of money for. Working in Hunt service you have a definite ladder of progression which, although it will take a long time, you can be aiming at; and although working as a hunter groom has no particular point of ambition, it can provide a very pleasant, healthy and active life.

# Racing and Polo

There can be no more 'glamorous' work with horses than in racing. How many boys must have watched the Derby field sweep round Tattenham Corner into the straight at Epsom and imagined themselves sitting poised on the favourite, waiting to pounce at the right moment; how many of their parents have watched the same scene and imagined themselves training the winner, or leading him in, the proud owner! And from 1975 such daydreams, or rather the riding one, need no longer be a purely male preserve, for after a trial period of amateur races, girls are now allowed to ride as professionals. On the flat, that is; riding in National Hunt races is still, as yet, regarded as too dangerous for the 'weaker sex', although I imagine it is only a matter of time before that barrier, too, is broken.

But there is a long gap between the desire to go into racing and having a ride of any sort in public, if indeed that ever does happen. There is virtually only one way that a school-leaver can go into racing and that is as an apprentice jockey, with the accent on 'apprentice'. When first you go into a racing stable you will be lucky to do much more than see a horse: mucking out, sweeping the yard, all the most menial tasks, but jobs which have to be well done, will most likely be your lot for the first few weeks. Only after a while, when you have shown a certain amount of reliability and commonsense, may you be given a horse or two to 'do'. These will be 'your' horses, as much as though you really did own them; and probably you will have at least as much affection for them, hope for them, worry about them, as the man who is paying the bills.

The sort of progress you make in a racing stable will to a very large extent depend upon yourself, on your ability, your determination, your resilience, because no matter how many good days you have you will also have plenty of bad ones, and you must be able to bounce back, both physically and mentally.

There is one thing you will not be able to do much about, of course, and that is your physique; the days have gone when boys were riding winners at 4–5st, but even now you need to be reasonably sure that, when you are fully grown, you will be able to ride at around 8st without having to go through the nerve- and body-wracking tortures of perpetual diet. There are exceptions, people who might normally be considered too big but who by sheer will-power keep their weight down. Lester Piggott is a supreme example; Jimmy Lindley, who retired not long ago, actually gave up riding at one time because of increasing weight until, with help and his own self-discipline, he conquered the problem. But jockeys such as these are rare indeed, and if you have the same sort of iron determination then the odds are that you will not even be bothering to read this, that you will have already made up your mind which is not to be changed by any theoretical snags.

No paper qualifications are needed to go into racing, and to get a job in a stable you need not necessarily even know how to ride. Some trainers prefer it that way, saying that anything a youngster may have learned in a riding school will be quite different from what is expected of him in racing; but for the most part some experience, even if it is only knowing how to muck out properly and how to go among horses quietly, without fuss and noise, will be welcomed. Thoroughbreds are unlike any other sort of horse – or perhaps one should say there is no sort of horse like a thoroughbred. As you may well know, all thoroughbreds in the General Stud Book are descended from just three stallions, the Byerley Turk, the Godolphin Arabian and the Darley Arabian, all of them imported from the Middle East but bred and reared selectively so that now the 'direct' descendants of the Arabian horses would have no chance of matching the modern thoroughbred for speed.

It has long been a matter for dispute, and will probably continue to be so, whether or not horses are intelligent, but thoroughbreds have more than their share of whatever intelligence, instinct – call it what you will – that is going. They are athletic and courageous, with greater powers of stamina and recuperation than horses of commoner blood; but because of this they need more delicate handling. Where some horses will give way to rough handling and bullying the thoroughbred, more likely than not, will rebel, and also, race-horses, if male, are probably entire horses – that is they have not been gelded –

which makes them prouder and less inclined to submit. Moreover, in training they will be well corned up, fit and full of youthful exuberance, ready and waiting for the odd prank. This may result in dropping their rider, you perhaps, heavily on to the ground, with who knows what result; or even causing themselves harm which, believe me, unless or until you are a Lester Piggott, will matter much more to the trainer than anything that may happen to you.

So when you are given your first horses to do they will not be the stars of the stable; maybe an 'old 'un' who is kept to lead the youngsters on to the gallops, perhaps the trainer's hack – who might himself be a pensioned-off favourite of the stable – or, if it is a smaller, mixed stable, possibly a hunter or a National Hunt horse who has gained commonsense, or a bit of native cunning, with the passing years. And when, finally, you are given your first ride, it will most likely be on a pony especially kept for the job, who would not win the Derby if he were given eleven furlongs start, but who will not get upset as you mess him around while you discover what to do with your hands or feet. If you do not make too much of a mess of this initial training then, later rather than sooner, you will get the chance you have been waiting for.

There are a lot of men in racing – 'lads' even though they may be old enough to be a grandfather – who are quite happy doing their two, knowing that the excitement, the glamour of riding into the winner's enclosure is not for them. But very few go into racing feeling that way; for the majority that ambition, that dream, is what it is all about, and the statistics, the knowledge that of the hundreds who go into racing only tens even get a ride in public, and of those a mere handful reach the top, mean absolutely nothing.

You will be up at the crack of dawn, or before it, getting your horse, 'your' horse, ready for work. And maybe it will be nothing more exciting than walk, walk, walk; but the pace will increase as the horse gets fitter and ready for the racecourse. Then, when he is ready, you will go with him; and even if you do have a pang of disappointment when you see someone else swing up into the saddle and walk him out on to the course, you will reassure yourself with the thought that one day that someone else may be you.

Riding is not all of it, of course, not by a long way. You will be expected to look after your horses in the stable more attentively than any mother hen ever did. The trainer and his head lad, if they are conscientious, will make their regular rounds of potential Derby winners and selling platers alike, but they are no more than human, probably overworked and trying to do three things at once, so that they may miss something: a slight listlessness, a disinclination to eat up, a touch of heat in a leg, a portent of misfortune to come which may well be avoided, or at least cut short, if the signs are seen in time. If you can show that you are alert enough to spot them and point them out you will have proved that you have an important part to play in what is inevitably a team effort – winning races.

Until very recently the way into a racing stable was for the father, school-master or whoever, of a boy about to leave school, small of stature with no particular scholastic bent, to write to a local trainer and ask if he had a place. If, at an interview, the trainer liked the boy's disposition in he would come, on the understanding that he would be kicked out equally quickly if he did not do as he was told. That is still quite often the way, but there is now an alternative and, if there can be such a thing in the world of horses, a short cut via the Apprentice Jockeys Scheme, financed by the Levy Board and run at the National Equestrian Centre at Stoneleigh, Warwickshire, the headquar-ters of the British Horse Society who act as agents for the board in the running of the scheme. The centre, with its indoor school, stabling and new hostel for accommodating the boys and girls, is ideally situated for this scheme, and indeed for other training schemes.

The scheme started several years ago under Major George Boon, a one-time show jumper who also acted as chef d'équipe for the British show jumping team for a while before getting more and more involved in racing, especially in the administrative side of racecourses, so that in 1974 he was appointed Clerk of the Course at both Doncaster and Aintree – the first man to hold the position simultaneously at the two courses where the famous 'Spring Double' races are run. Then the scheme was switched to Stoneleigh and a former jockey, Johnnie Gilbert, brought in as trainer.

Johnnie Gilbert was apprenticed as a boy to Stanley Wootton at Epsom, one of the finest trainers of riders as well as horses, who was also responsible for the rise of such men as Staff Ingham, Ron Smyth and 'Frenchie' Nicholson, all of them now trainers and the last-named generally rated as one of the top producers of talented young riders. This suggests that training trainers is an ability that can be learned just as well as training horses by those who take the bother to do so. Gilbert rode on the flat and then over hurdles – an art at which he was a master – and with his temperament, patient and good-humoured but not a man to be taken advantage of, he was an ideal choice for the job of train-ing prospective young jockeys. Like Nicholson, he believes in the 'carrot' rather than the 'stick' in encouraging youngsters; not ignoring their mistakes, but pointing them out in a friendly, constructive sort of way rather than bel-lowing at them as, alas, some trainers do. The result is that in the seven weeks which is all these courses last he often works minor miracles, taking boys who have never ridden before and sending them out able to ride gallops as well as having a rudimentary knowledge of stable routine.

To start with these courses, aimed at bringing boys into a job which was getting dangerously understaffed because of the easier hours and greater pay of rival occupations, were confined to boys already in racing stables, but trainers' understandable reluctance to part with what help they had got, meant that fewer boys were taking advantage of it than had been hoped.

The British Horse Society suggested to the Levy Board that it might be advantageous to take boys and girls straight from school, and this has, in a comparatively short time, proved a success. The names of likely candidates are sent by local careers offices to Brigadier Henry Green at the Horserace Betting Levy Board, 17/23 Southampton Row, London WC2, and Brigadier Green and a selection panel then interview them at Stoneleigh and make their choice. Six courses are held each year, each of seven weeks duration, with about ten boys or girls on each; the scheme is still in its infancy but probably there will continue to be six courses with four for boys and two for girls, although Johnnie Gilbert makes no secret of the fact that if he had his way the proportion would be the other way around, as he finds girls easier to teach, better behaved and more conscientious.

Although there is, perhaps inevitably, a fairly high wastage, since the majority of those going into the course have no first-hand idea of what is involved, it is estimated that around forty youngsters a year are now going into racing able to make a useful contribution from the day they join their stable.

Johnnie Gilbert, instructor to the apprentice jockeys at the National Equestrian Centre, swops his horse for a bicycle as he supervises a course of girl apprentices riding out

Generally speaking the boys, when they have finished the course at Stoneleigh, are placed in stables in the area they come from, so that the wrench of leaving home is not so great and they have the chance of returning fairly often. It is a sad irony that the scheme should have got under way so effectively at a time when, because of the declining economic situation, stables are tending to cut down on the number of horses they keep and the number of lads needed to look after them; but one can only hope that this is a passing phase, and in any case those who have had some training will obviously be preferred to those with none.

The apprentice courses at Stoneleigh are aimed at producing youngsters for flat-race stables, because clearly it is difficult enough, in just seven weeks, to get a boy or girl who has maybe never ridden at all before to ride gallops let alone to jump; and in any case Johnnie Gilbert, even if he were given a longer time, prefers it this way. There is plenty of time for them to learn to ride over fences and hurdles when they have a great deal more experience. Nevertheless, some boys may go into a National Hunt stable, and the procedure is very much the same. Obviously it would be an advantage if a boy had ridden a bit, perhaps hunted; many of the top National Hunt riders started as amateurs and then turned professional when they were successful, people such as Terry Biddle-combe or Bill Smith, while one of the best of the younger jockeys, John Fran-come, was a highly successful show jumper and reached international status as a junior before joining the stable of Fred Winter, arguably the greatest NH jockey of all and now equally successful as a trainer. But if you go in as an apprentice, given the luck, talent and determination, it is just as possible to be successful and, within reason, a light weight is not so vitally important riding 'over the sticks'.

Of course it may be that, for one reason or another, an apprentice does not make the grade as a jockey; as I have already said, the odds are very much against it. Even so, working in a racing stable can be an interesting and exciting life. The aim of most, with riding ambitions behind them, is to become Head Lad – a vital job whose importance is in direct ratio to the knowledge and experience of the trainer. The Head Lad is a trainer's right-hand man, responsible for much of the day-to-day running of a stable, the feeding and general welfare of the horses. It takes many years and a lot of experience before one is ready for such a job; the trainer should feel that he can go away, perhaps for several days, knowing that the routine which is vital to a successful stable will carry on in his absence, with someone there quite capable of dealing with the problems that are bound to occur from time to time. As well as being able to look after the horses a Head Lad has to be able to 'look after' the staff, lads and apprentices; as in any close-knit community, small squabbles and petty jealousies can blow up into arguments out of all proportion to their cause without a firm, fair hand to deal with them, and that sort of atmosphere in a racing stable would be disastrous.

Almost as important is the Travelling Head Lad, whose job, as the title explains, is to travel with the horses to their races and look after them there. Often there are particular difficulties involved – some horses do not like travelling, or do not like being stabled overnight away from home, and can get so upset that months of work preparing for a certain race can be fretted away in the last few hours. Sometimes, too, the Travelling Head Lad will have to stand in for the trainer at the racecourse, making sure that the horse is a declared runner for his race, that the jockey who has been engaged has arrived at the course, attending to a dozen little things any one of which, omitted or badly done, can make the difference between victory and defeat, even between running and not running.

Of course there are other specialist jobs about the stable too, such as box-driving; although many stables prefer to hire boxes, especially if they are in a thriving training area, rather than have the bother and worry of maintaining their own. And one of the most important men in the 'team' is the trainer's secretary, whose tasks can cover everything from the accounts – a highly complex business – to the entries, correspondence with owners, dealing with potential owners, and generally taking over the 'paperwork' so that the trainer can get on with the job of training the horses.

This, clearly, is not the sort of job that someone just leaving school could think about; like so many other jobs in racing it would inevitably go to someone who already knew quite a lot about the sport if only because a trainer would not have the time, and probably not the inclination, to teach his secretary the many different facets of this most fascinating of sports. But there are jobs open to someone with good secretarial training and an interest in, rather than much knowledge of, racing: possibly with Weatherbys who are official secretaries to the Jockey Club and have been for many years, with a responsibility for dealing with race entries, for producing the Racing Calendar each week, and a great deal more; or with the Horserace Betting Levy Board; or again maybe with one of the bloodstock agencies, who are dealt with more fully later. The Racing Information Bureau, at 42 Portman Square, London W1H 0JE may well be able to help you.

There are a lot of other jobs in racing, such as the running of racecourses, including the stipendary stewards, or handicapping, although this is now done increasingly on a computerised basis, but these are invariably performed by people with a knowledge of racing, quite possibly former riders. It is just, as well as sensible, that this should be so, for riding, even for the most successful, is a fairly short-lived career and not many jockeys make enough to be able to retire afterwards. Quite a lot, of course, take up training, but success at one is by no means a guarantee of success at the other; the devil-may-care dash needed to win races as a rider may be a stronger element in a man's make-up than the patience and attention to detail that is necessary to produce the same result as a trainer.

In racing, more perhaps than in any other equestrian activity except possibly hunting, jobs tend to be kept 'in the family', handed down from father to son; not for any particularly nepotic reasons but because racing is not so much a career as a way of life. It becomes, to those bitten by it, wholly engrossing in all its aspects: breeding horses, which is covered in another section, training and riding them, organising the races and running them – racing is one of the major spectator sports – and betting on them, which is another job that may interest you. So much so that few men who have been involved in racing willingly leave it. It is a sport with a tremendous tradition but it is also one in which ability matters most; you may be the son of a Duke, but if the son of a dustman rides better he will be the one that owners and trainers want for their horses. The old saying that 'On the turf and under it all men are equal' is possibly even more true now than when it was written.

So if you do feel the urge to go into racing – and do not unless the urge is strong for it is a hard, highly competitive life – then you can do so in the knowledge that, given a little luck, it will be up to you how well you do, and in these restrictive days that is surely worth a lot.

## Polo

Virtually the only way that one can work with polo ponies professionally is as a groom; the chance of making a living out of riding them is slight. Even as a groom this is very much a seasonal occupation, for the polo season lasts from April until the end of August or the beginning of September, and even given a few weeks before the start of competition to get ponies fit and ready the work still lasts, for the most part, for only about half a year.

Having said which, this is undoubtedly a very pleasant sort of work with horses. It is a fairly static occupation, in that most owners of polo ponies are based at one particular club; their ponies stay there and so of course do the grooms, except for an occasional visit, for a weekend perhaps, to another club. Mostly the games are played in the afternoon – although there are also some evening matches – so that the hours of work are reasonable, with none of the very early hours that are needed in a hunting stable.

Polo has become an increasingly popular game over the past few years, with a lot of encouragement for youngsters, and is played in the Pony Club, so it is

Polo at Windsor

quite possible to get a taste for it before you leave school, to find out what it is all about and to have some experience of riding polo ponies, which naturally will stand you in good stead when you come to work with them. The ponies themselves are well-trained – they have to be for the work that they are called upon to perform – usually with a good temperament and also, although there is no longer a height limit (at the turn of the century there was a height limit of 14·2 hands, but this was abolished in 1916), they are smaller than the average hunter and therefore more suitable for young and small girls. It is a matter of opinion what is the optimum height for a polo pony but the general consensus is about 15·3–16hh.

Polo is one of the oldest of games and was played in Persia before 600 BC. It was also played in India, from whence it was introduced to Britain by some officers who had served there in 1869. It is one of the fastest of games and makes such demands on the ponies playing it that a game has to be divided into short sessions – chukkas – of seven and a half minutes each, between which the ponies are changed. Although there are strict rules to prevent 'dangerous' play, the game itself is intrinsically hazardous and rough, and a pony would be lucky indeed to go for long without a few bumps and scrapes; so that anyone looking after polo ponies would obviously be very much more useful if he or she had a rudimentary veterinary knowledge.

Polo training: getting the swing right at an indoor school before going out to put it into practice

There is no statutory requirement as to the breed of polo ponies but there is a considerable bias in favour of the Argentine criollo crossed with thoroughbred; the resulting animals tend to combine hardiness with speed and agility, a good temperament and intelligence. These qualities are invaluable, not only on the polo field: one of the most famous of three-day event horses, Princess Anne's Doublet, was bred by the Queen by Doubtless III, a winner of the Argentine Triple Crown, from a polo pony mare, Swaté.

It is not only the ponies who come from the Argentine; a large number of players do also, not only to Britain but to France, Spain and Italy, and also to India and Pakistan. They are almost the only professionals apart from grooms. Often they come with strings of ponies, are paid for playing and then sell their ponies and return home to reappear the next season with more ponies. Until World War II polo was essentially an amateur game, and there was a rule that no player could be paid to play; this was changed after the war, hence the increasing number of Argentine players. They have the additional advantage of bringing trained ponies, because finding the men to train polo ponies is a difficulty in this country. Theoretically it would be possible for someone with sufficient capital to buy the right sort of ponies, train and sell them, but it would be a considerable gamble.

To try to make a living out of being paid to play, a boy, or girl, although her chances would be even more remote, would first have to prove his ability in the saddle; this alone could be difficult enough, for players of even quite moderate ability would, generally speaking, rather go on playing themselves to a good age than pay someone else to ride their ponies. There are only some 200 openings for professional riders in this country, so clearly the competition is keen. Even if you were lucky enough to be paid to play, it would only be for the season, after which you would need to play abroad – as a career prospect it is obviously very limited.

If you are keen to play polo it might be possible to work as a groom; you would get riding exercise and training, with the chance of playing occasionally. This is apparently a growing trend in the United States where grooms, when they are good enough, are paid extra for playing.

To sum up, working with polo ponies can be a pleasant occupation during the summer and, although the living conditions may be on the primitive side, the people involved tend to be likeable; but it is essentially a groom's job and a seasonal one. The ruling body of the sport in this country is the Hurlingham Polo Association, whose secretary is Brigadier J. R. C. Gannon, 60 Mark Lane, London EC3R 7TJ.

# Studs – Horses and Ponies

If working with horses, rather than riding them, is what appeals to you, then there can be no more pleasant, rewarding and utterly satisfying life than on a stud farm; and these vary sufficiently to be able to accommodate just about every inclination. There are the famous thoroughbred studs which produce the horses that race in this country and which may also be sold abroad and make a valuable contribution to the country's economy; the smaller, private thoroughbred studs; the studs such as those which house the Hunters' Improvement Society's premium stallions, which produce half-breds for hunting, show jumping, showing and so much else; and the studs for the native pony breeds, which can be a fine way for a beginner to start a career in breeding and is sufficiently different and self-contained, under the aegis of the National Pony Society, to warrant a separate section at the end of this chapter. You would probably be best advised to begin your stud career at a smaller establishment and perhaps widen your experience at more than one before you settle.

Thoroughbred breeding is very big business; each year millions of pounds' worth of horses are sold at public auction in Britain alone, quite apart from private sales, or those which are kept to race. It is also a subject on which there are almost as many different ideas as there are people involved; differences of opinion on the theory of breeding and on the value of the many different bloodlines, so that, for example, the great Italian, Federico Tesio, was able to introduce into Italy horses that were generally regarded as only moderate, and therefore inexpensive, and from them, working to his own ideas, produce a succession of horses of world-beating class like Ribot; differences, too, in rearing, though these have tended to become more standardised as knowledge increases and veterinary science advances. Because thoroughbreds finally face the acid test of competition on the racecourse, the most revolutionary ideas can be attempted and the final arbiter is not what men say but which is the winning racehorse.

No matter how well bred a horse may be, and no matter how well trained, if he is not properly cared for in his early days all the expense and effort will come to nought. There is, inevitably, a considerable element of luck about breeding racehorses: how often it happens that the same parents in the same environment breed two brothers, one a champion, the other unable to win even one race. This is accepted, and regarded by some as part of the thrill of it, but it is the responsibility of a stud staff, from the owner or manager down, to ensure that this fateful chance is kept to a minimum and that every foal born into their care is given the chance to thrive and grow strong and ready for the fray. Which is not to say that he, or she, need be as overweight as some youngsters are when sent up for public auction to give an illusion of being bigger and better than they really are.

Despite all that will eventually depend upon the studgroom, there are no particular qualifications demanded nor any course of training to be followed at the outset of his career. A youngster who is interested must apply to a stud and then, if accepted, will learn the job from the older, more experienced members of the staff; even more than with most jobs with horses, it is one that demands patience and attention to detail to a considerable degree. Professor William Miller, former director of the Equine Research Station at Newmarket, has written a most excellent book, *Practical Essentials in the Care and Management of Horses on Thoroughbred Studs*, which was published a decade or so ago by the Thoroughbred Breeders' Association, and one especial point he makes is that 'young studsmen should take every opportunity to study every animal under their care as thoroughly as possible. No two mares, foals or yearlings are ever alike in behaviour, temperament or reactions and the more knowledge of their varying characteristics the studsman possesses the better he can manage them and make necessary allowances for different individuals.'

The book is all its title implies; from notes on pastures and buildings, through the handling of horses, management of mares, foals and stallions, notes on disease and hygiene, on feeding and watering.

As a studgroom you will meet many problems that those involved in the riding, training or grooming of horses will not; eventually, for instance, you

Mares and foals being led out to their paddock

will probably have to handle stallions. They have a reputation for wildness, for being difficult to handle but, like any other horses, they vary, and a stallion which has been trained firmly but kindly should be perfectly tractable. Normally this would be a man's rather than a woman's job because of the strength involved, but the strongest man who tried to pit himself against a horse would find himself in trouble. And it is, though rare, not unknown for a stallion to be quite amenable to dividing his time between covering mares and being ridden out hunting, or show jumping or eventing.

You will also have to care for the youngstock, and with them especially will need a keen, observant eye so that, after years of experience, you may be able to tell almost by instinct if all is not well and whether the problem is serious enough to warrant calling the vet, or if it is something that you, or possibly the studgroom, can deal with. Gradually you will gain knowledge and experience, and may well be able to attend one of the courses that the Thoroughbred Breeders' Association arranges at intervals; each year they have one, run in conjunction with the Equine Research Station at Newmarket, for studmen, studgrooms or stud owners and/or managers. The syllabus for the latest one for studmen will give some idea of the scope both of the course and of the sort of work you will be doing. The six-day course covers:

*Anatomy* – alimentary system; reproductive system.

*Physiology* – foodstuffs, quality and choice; growth and feeding.

*Pathology* – laboratory aspects of acute infections in the young foal; parasites and control of worms; congenital and other deformities of foals.

*Clinical* – care of feet and shoeing, including farriery; lameness; disinfection on the stud; management of stallions; first aid on studs; care of the foal before and after birth; diseases of foals; fostering of orphan foals; foaling, care and management of mare and foals at foaling; disease resistance and immunity in the newborn; haemolytic disease; colic; respiratory disease; abortion.

*Conformation* – conformation, including anatomy of bones, ligaments and muscles.

*Demonstrations* – laboratory demonstrations; visit to National Stud; preparation for sale, Stetchworth Park Stud; trying and covering, Egerton Stud; grassland management and poisonous plants; the Jockey Club Rooms.

The courses arranged by the TBA are confined to their members and members' employees. The one for owners and managers is, naturally, most comprehensive, and if you should have ambitions of one day at least managing a stud if not owning one the syllabus of the most recent course will show what is involved:

*Anatomy* – limbs, bones, ligaments and muscles; alimentary system; reproductive system.

*Physiology* – cardiovascular and respiratory system; growth and feeding; principles of feeding; botanical aspects of grassland; grassland demonstrations.

*Pathology* – epidemiology on the stud; laboratory demonstrations; factors influencing the development of illness; parasitology; congenital and other deformities of foals; the pathology and laboratory aspects of abortion.

*Clinical* – hygiene and disinfection on the stud; healing of wounds; antiseptics, antibiotics; management of stallions; first aid on studs; care of foals before and after birth; foaling, care and management of mare and foal; diseases of foals; haemolytic diseases; blood groups; colic (and after-care after surgery); respiratory disease; practical aspect of abortion; trying and covering; care of the feet.

*General* – conformation; planned breeding; stud farm accounts; stud book procedure and documentation; the analytical chemist and racing.

*Demonstrations* – National Stud (including preparation of animals for sale); Beech House Stud; Egerton Stud (including demonstration of trying and covering); Derisley Wood Stud; Clinical department, Equine Research Station; Peter E. Burrell laboratories for haematology and chemical pathology.

Night-watchmen at the National Stud, Newmarket, keeping an eye on mares about to foal

One of the most important aspects of successful breeding is the land upon which the stud is situated and its condition. The Equine Research Station, a department of the Animal Health Trust which was founded in 1942, has what is possibly a unique 'testing ground' for all varieties and various mixtures of grass, arranged in sections so that the trials really can be held 'in the field'.

Each season the National Stud accepts four or five young men as trainee students, usually preferring those who are likely eventually to own or manage studs; they only take men with experience, who join the staff in an unpaid capacity except for free board and lodging, so that they can take time off for lectures, demonstrations, etc, away from the stud. They stay for the duration of the breeding season – February to June inclusive – but applications have to be made at least six months in advance and be supported with recommendations. The National Stud was founded in 1915 when Colonel Hall Walker offered his bloodstock at Tully, Co Kildare, Ireland, to the British Government; Tully was sold to the Irish Government in 1943, the National Stud transferred to Gillingham in Dorset and in 1960 it was decided to build a National Stud at Newmarket. Mr Peter Burrell, who had been director of the stud since 1937, was able to plan the stud literally from scratch, and the result, which was officially opened by Her Majesty the Queen in 1967, is a model stud at which some of the most famous and successful of British stallions stand.

The stud concentrates on keeping stallions rather than having mares of its own, the idea being to preserve for British breeders the top stallions rather than compete with them commercially by keeping mares and breeding foals for sale. The majority of smaller thoroughbred studs tend to keep mares, possibly with one stallion, but quite likely sending the mares to stallions at other studs: it would be a hazardous policy, however, to send all one's mares to the same stallion for season after season.

As with other jobs with horses, there is no reason why you should confine your activities to this country; thoroughbred breeding is carried out in many parts of the world – the interchange of bloodstock has been widespread, especially in the past two or three decades – and although different environments will demand differing techniques to a certain extent, an experienced studman will always find employment.

As well as directing the National Stud for many years, until his retirement in 1975, Lieutenant Colonel Douglas Gray plays an important advisory part in the running of one of the most important breeding organisations in the country – the Hunters' Improvement and National Light Horse Breeding Society. Where the TBA is primarily involved in producing horses to race, the HIS has as its main function raising the general level of horses throughout the country, be they hunters, event horses, show jumpers, sometimes racehorses, or just common-or-garden riding horses. Each March the HIS holds a stallion show at Newmarket, at which stallions are judged and selected to stand in certain areas, which collectively cover the country. The society pays premiums to the owners of these stallions from a grant given by the Levy Board so that the fee paid by members of the society can be kept down.

Working at a stud where a premium stallion, or possibly several such stallions, stands would involve contact with possibly a wider section of the horse world than in one that was exclusively thoroughbred. Whatever you may choose, stud work is always fascinating; and while not as hectic as ridden work, it can be just as difficult, frustrating at times, and equally fulfilling. Possibly even more so, for while it is satisfactory to see a horse one has trained do well in its particular sphere, how much more so with a horse for whose very existence one is responsible.

## Ponies

Most people start riding on ponies and retain an affection for them long after they have graduated to horses. The very qualities which make ponies ideal for learning to ride – their small size, their basically kind temperament – make them also a fine starting point for a career with horses, although for many people ponies are not a stepping-stone to the bigger animals but a wholly satisfying end in themselves.

Working with ponies covers a very similar spectrum to working with horses, with no need for duplication here, but there is some specialisation, in particular connected with the breeding and showing of ponies. The ruling body in this country is the National Pony Society, whose address is 85 Cliddesden Road, Basingstoke, Hants RG21 3HA, who are only too willing to give help and advice to anyone contemplating a career with ponies, or to anyone so engaged who has a particular problem. Each year the National Pony Society holds a show at which many of the finest ponies in the country are brought together in competition, and a most attractive show it is.

What are known as the Mountain and Moorland ponies are those indigenous to the British Isles, who have from ages past made their homes in the respective areas which give them their names, and have developed particular characteristics. In many cases they still live in a wild state; the breeds are Welsh, Shetland, Dartmoor, New Forest, Highland, Exmoor, Fell, Dales and Connemara. Over the years there have been 'transfusions' of other blood, Arab and Hackney for example, into some of the breeds, but the native characteristics are very jealously guarded and the resulting ponies are much in demand all over the world. In addition there are what are loosely known as riding ponies, which describes no specific breed but rather a type; these can vary from the working pony who may be no great beauty but can go out hunting, take part in gymkhanas or work in riding schools, to the aristocrats of the show ring – sometimes miniature thoroughbreds, although this may well differ according to the current fashion among judges, dealers and breeders.

The majority of pony studs tend to be run on fairly small lines with a few mares and possibly one stallion, although more likely they will visit a stallion. Because these are very often family businesses, if indeed they are businesses at all rather than totally absorbing hobbies on the part of the owners, there is much more likelihood of a beginner being able to find employment in them when a thoroughbred stud will be looking for someone with a certain amount of experience.

The NPS awards diplomas at two levels, both of which make provision for those for whom riding is not an important part. To be able to take the examination as a Stud Assistant the candidate must be at least sixteen years old and have had one year's experience or more in a reputable stud. The examination for this covers:

1 *Breeding*
  Candidates must have had experience of handling a pony stallion.
  Foaling, weaning, the handling and management of brood mares, the rearing and handling of youngstock, both in stable and at grass.
  Candidates must have seen a mare foal or a film showing this.
2 *Breaking*
  Candidates should be able to assess the stage of training which an animal has reached.
  Candidates must be capable of exercising a young and/or fit animal up to 15·2hh competently.
  Candidates must be able to lunge a pony correctly.
3 *Riding*
  Candidates will be examined in riding and should be active and effective horsemen, able to apply seat, legs and hands efficiently.
  Candidates should be capable of riding an unknown pony and able to teach a pony the aids.
  Part of the ridden examination must be on a not fully schooled animal.
  The 'Impression of Horsemanship and Competence' must be written with marks by the examiners in all phases.
  The standard for Stud Assistant should be similar to Pony Club B test as far as riding is concerned.
  Every candidate will be asked to ride without stirrups.
  Candidates must have a basic knowledge of how and what a horse can jump at the specific stage of its training.
4 *Pony/stable management*
  Feeding and forage, watering, bedding, exercise, grooming, clipping and trimming, theory of shoeing, care of saddlery; elementary veterinary knowledge and treatment.

*5 Show production and presentation*
The production and presentation of ponies, including Mountain and Moorland ponies, for showing in hand, and their transportation.


Section 3 may be omitted in which case the successful candidate would receive a Stable Assistant (Non Riding) Diploma.

The NPS Diploma in Pony Mastership and Breeding is intended as a guarantee of a high standard of knowledge and ability and a minimum of eighty per cent is required in all subjects. Again one year's experience, at least, in a reputable stud is required, and the candidate must be at least twenty-one years old. The examination for this covers·


*1 Breeding*
Covering, foaling, weaning, the handling and management of pony stallions, the handling and management of broodmares, the rearing and handling of youngstock, both in stable and at grass.

Candidates must have sufficient knowledge to be capable of caring for a mare that has developed complications at foaling time, until a veterinary surgeon is available.

*2 Breaking*
Candidates must know the theory and practice of breaking a young pony from the start up to a standard at which it is capable of being hunted, including lungeing, long reining, mouthing, bits and bitting, backing, obedience, jumping.

*3 Pony/stable management*
Feeding and forage, watering, bedding, exercise, grooming, clipping and trimming; thorough knowledge of shoeing; care of saddlery.
Veterinary knowledge and treatment.

*4 Show production and presentation*
The production and presentation of ponies, including Mountain and Moorland ponies, for showing in hand and under saddle, and their transportation.

*5 Riding*
Candidates will be examined in riding and should be active and effective horsemen, able to apply seats, legs and hands efficiently.

Candidates should be capable of riding an unknown pony; able to teach a pony the aids.

The standard of riding to be not lower than that of Pony Club A test.

Alternative for the Non Riding Diploma:

5 *Agricultural management of stud land*
Fencing, grass management, grazing, eradication of parasites, watering, land draining, gate fastening, mineral test of soil, spraying, fertilisers.

These examinations are held at various establishments throughout the country, details of which can be obtained from the National Pony Society, who will also supply a list of recommended studs to which anyone who wishes to make a career with ponies could apply. If you go as a working pupil then clearly you cannot expect to be paid, or at least no more than pocket money with your food and lodging provided. The precise arrangements must, as always, be something you, and possibly your parents, make with the stud concerned but, as has been said before, working with ponies or horses is not something to be done for the financial rewards and it is important to look at your arrangements for where they will lead and how much you will learn rather than for how much you will earn.

With experience and knowledge you will have no difficulty in finding employment either at home or overseas, especially, perhaps, in North America where British ponies are so popular.

# Veterinary Surgery

Most children who like animals have a daydream at some time or another of being a veterinary surgeon. Like all the medical professions it has a glamour about it; with visions of wandering, white-coated, around the countryside curing sick and wounded animals, almost effortlessly. In reality veterinary work is a long way from this; it requires a very high standard of education even before one can start to study for a veterinary degree. Moreover, when one is qualified the work is often hard – more so in many cases than when treating people because an animal cannot tell you what is wrong – and often in the sort of conditions that would make a doctor, used to working in a hospital or surgery, throw up his hands in horror.

But although the road to becoming a vet is a long and hard one, the goal can be infinitely rewarding, and varied too. A qualified and registered veterinary surgeon may work in private practice – this accounts for more than half of those currently registered – either as partners or assistants in multiple practices, or as single-handed practitioners, although these are comparatively rare. The type of work that a private vet is involved in would, to a very large extent, depend upon the location of his practice: if it is in a town then, clearly, the majority of the cases he would be called upon to deal with would be small domestic animals, dogs, cats, rabbits, cage birds and the like; if in the country, there would be much more demand for his services in connection with farm animals, poultry, horses, etc. Most practices are mixed and deal with all kinds of animals, but some veterinary surgeons specialise, and those who specialise in horses have banded together to form the British Equine Veterinary Association as a division of the British Veterinary Association.

Roughly one seventh of the 6,000 or so veterinary surgeons active in Britain are employed in government research or field service. This research, which also covers government-sponsored research agencies, may be either pure or applied research; the field service is chiefly involved with the control of diseases which are prevalent among livestock farming or which are important to public health.

Teaching and research in universities employs about five per cent of vets in this country; an increasing number are engaged in commercial research and in advisory capacities with pharmaceutical and animal feed companies. There is also, frequently, the opportunity to work overseas, mainly in Commonwealth countries. A recent announcement from the Royal College of Veterinary Surgeons stated that there is a marked shortage of veterinary graduates in the United Kingdom, although there is a surplus in some EEC countries.

The Royal College of Veterinary Surgeons is the 'ruling body' of the profession in Great Britain and Ireland. The first veterinary college in these islands was opened in London in 1791, with a French veterinary surgeon, St Bel, from Lyons, as its professor; in 1823 William Dick founded the second veterinary school, in Edinburgh. The graduates of the two schools, intent on maintaining a high standard in the profession, joined together – there were about a thousand of them at the time – to petition Queen Victoria for a royal charter, incorporating them as the Royal College of Veterinary Surgeons. This was granted in 1844, and the charter declared that only members of the college should be 'individually known and distinguished by the name or title of Veterinary Surgeon'. Further royal charters extending the powers of the college have been granted since, the latest in 1967.

For more than 100 years after the granting of the royal charter of 1844 the RCVS itself examined all veterinary students who had studied at the schools in London, Edinburgh, Glasgow (founded in 1862), Liverpool (founded in Edinburgh in 1873 and moved in 1900) and Dublin, where the Veterinary College of Ireland was founded in 1900.

The Veterinary Surgery Act of 1948 gave the responsibility for examining students to the universities; the universities now awarding a veterinary degree are London, Liverpool, Edinburgh, Glasgow, Bristol and Cambridge and, in Dublin, Trinity College and University College. The award of a veterinary degree is an automatic qualification for membership of the Royal College, which gives the right to practice veterinary surgery in the United Kingdom and the Irish Republic. Unqualified practice is illegal. Although no longer having the direct control it did before 1948, the RCVS retains a supervisory role over veterinary education.

The six universities in the UK which provide veterinary degree courses vary in the titles of their degrees, be they veterinary science, veterinary medicine or veterinary medicine and surgery, but all the degrees give the right to membership of the Royal College. Candidates for the universities must obviously satisfy the entrance requirements of the university concerned which, in general, would normally be five passes in approved subjects in GCE examinations, including passes in two approved subjects at A Level. Candidates for a veterinary course would also need to provide evidence that they are in a position to read the subjects of the course with profit; which would mean A Level passes in three subjects such as chemistry, physics and biology, or botany and zoology, but the precise requirements of a university can only be ascertained from the university itself.

It is an indication of the difficulty in obtaining a place on a veterinary degree course that there are usually three or four applicants for each available place.

Applications for places in most universities are made through the Universities Central Council on Admissions (UCCA), whose address is PO Box 28, Cheltenham, Gloucestershire GL50 1HY.

UCCA publish a booklet 'How to Apply for Admission to a University' each June, which is usually sent to schools, together with application forms for entry to university in October of the following year. The latest date for receipt by UCCA of applications for admission is 15 October for candidates including Cambridge among their choice and 15 December for candidates not including Cambridge in the year preceding that for which application for admission is being made. A prospective candidate for Cambridge should also apply directly to one of the colleges, and a candidate applying only to Glasgow should write not to UCCA but to the Registrar, University of Glasgow, Glasgow W2.

Would-be candidates for the Irish universities should write directly to them, but it should be noted that Trinity take no applicants from outside Ireland for their School of Veterinary Medicine.

Veterinary degree courses usually last for five years, but an undergraduate may interrupt his course for one or two years to take an honours course in a science subject such as anatomy, biochemistry, physiology or pathology. The courses at Cambridge take six years, but a student may specialise for one year.

To begin with a veterinary course would normally comprise subjects which deal with the structure and functions of an animal, such as anatomy, physiology and biochemistry, because such knowledge is essential for a proper understanding of both sick and healthy animals. Then the courses would develop with subjects which provide a knowledge of the nature of disease, such as pharmacology, pathology and bacteriology. After this clinical subjects, veterinary medicine, veterinary surgery and obstetrics, together with animal health and husbandry, and the control and prevention of disease, would be the main studies for the final part of the course.

As well as the studies at university, a graduate is expected to gain experience during the vacations: for a start this might be on a farm, getting general experience of working with animals; later he would have to spend six months, spread among several vacations, 'seeing practice'. This involves working with veterinary surgeons in general practice, in laboratory research and in connection with food hygiene and inspection.

The Royal College of Veterinary Surgeons publish a booklet called 'A Career as a Veterinary Surgeon', which can be obtained from them at 32 Belgrave Square, London SW1X 8QP, price 20p, which gives a great deal of detail, in particular of the courses of each university, but it may be of some use to give a few details of each here.

*Bristol* The course extends over five years of which the first three provide grounding in the basic veterinary sciences. These cover animal handling and animal management and include weekly visits to the Langford School for practical work. They lead on to the study of disease and animal husbandry and at the end of this period those achieving high enough placings have the opportunity to spend a year reading for an honours BSc degree in one of the subjects they have been studying. For the two final years, the clinical years, students are in residence at the Langford Veterinary School, some fourteen miles from Bristol. There are usually 150 veterinary undergraduates at one time, about 30 being admitted each year, of whom about 8 are usually girls.

*Cambridge* The veterinary courses at Cambridge are divided into two equal parts. The first three years deal with the basic preclinical sciences, taught within the framework of the Medical and Natural Sciences Triposes and lead to a BA degree. For the veterinary degree there follow three years of clinical study and instruction. There is a good deal of flexibility in the courses, for which some 30 places are reserved each year, although there may be more, with no restriction on the number of places which may be filled by girls. As has been said application should be made, as well as to UCCA, to the Admissions Tutor of a specific college before 1 September of the year before intended entry.

*Edinburgh*   The veterinary school of Edinburgh University is the Royal (Dick) School of Veterinary Studies, and the degree course lasts for five years. The first year is occupied with the study of anatomy, physiology and biochemistry; animal husbandry is studied in the second year, and in the third, veterinary microbiology, pathology and parasitology. The fourth year includes pharmacology and general therapeutics and clinical studies, and the final year courses are in veterinary medicine, surgery, obstetrics and reproduction, and also animal health and veterinary public health. There is a small animal practice in Edinburgh and a large one at the field station at Roslin, eight miles outside Edinburgh, where the latter years are spent. There are approximately 270 veterinary undergraduates at one time, with an annual intake of about 55 of whom 5 or 6 may be girls.

*Glasgow*   The course at Glasgow normally lasts for five years, but there is a possibility of reduction to four for well-qualified SCE and GCE students. The first year of the course covers the basic science subjects, and the second normal structure and function; the third year covers animal husbandry and veterinary pathology, which carries forward to the fourth year, integrated with courses in veterinary medicine, surgery and reproduction and veterinary pharmacology. This is in association with part-time teachers from the Veterinary Department of the Corporation of Glasgow, who are responsible for instruction in meat inspection and food hygiene. The fifth year covers the principles and practice of veterinary medicine surgery and reproduction. There are approximately 250 veterinary undergraduate students, with an annual intake to the first and second years of 50–55 students; the number of women students almost equals that of men.

*Liverpool*   The course is over five years, of which the first deals with anatomy and organic chemistry; the second and third cover physiology and biochemistry, pathology, parasitology and animal husbandry, and give an introduction to clinical studies. These are the main studies in the fourth and fifth years, together with veterinary preventive medicine, clinical pathology and food hygiene. The courses are held in Liverpool and at the field station at Leahurst, on the Wirral peninsula, where final year students are resident. There are usually between 180 and 200 veterinary students, with an annual intake of about 40, of whom about 9 are girls.

*London*   The Royal Veterinary College is the veterinary school of London University, and the course extends over four years and two terms. The teaching departments are grouped into three parts: preclinical studies, paraclinical

studies and clinical studies. Courses in the first two years cover preclinical subjects, as well as instruction in animal management and animal husbandry
during the first three terms. After passing the first examination students begin
the paraclinical and clinical studies, which comprise pathology, animal health
and reproduction, surgery and obstetrics, clinical and experimental medicine.
These courses are held partly in the college buildings in Camden Town and
partly at the field station near North Mimms, Hertfordshire, where final year
students may be in residence. There are approximately 300 veterinary students
at one time, with 65 admitted annually, of whom about 15 or 16 may be girls.

The two Dublin Universities confine their veterinary courses to Irish resi-
dents. Information can be obtained by writing to the School of Veterinary
Medicine, University of Dublin, Trinity College, Ballsbridge, Dublin 4.

Local education authorities in England, Wales and Northern Ireland are
able to make grants for all suitably qualified students accepted for first degrees
at universities in the United Kingdom, and student allowances are similarly
made in Scotland by the Scottish Education Department. In addition some
awards are made by universities, details of which may be obtained from the
universities themselves. Entrance scholarships are awarded at all the Cambridge colleges, and include the D.O. Morgan Scholarship at St Catharine's
College, which is open only to those who wish to read veterinary medicine.

Assistance towards the payment of fees of students at Scottish universities
may be given to applicants of Scottish birth, extraction or schooling by the
Carnegie Trust. Regulations and application forms may be had from the Secretary and Treasurer, The Carnegie Trust for the Universities of Scotland, The
Merchant Hall, 22 Hanover Street, Edinburgh 2. Completed application forms
should be lodged by 20 October.

The Animal Health Trust may make loans to students who have completed
part of their veterinary course satisfactorily and find themselves in financial
difficulty. Particulars may be had from the Animal Health Trust, 24 Portland
Place, London W1N 4HN.

The Fitzwygram, Lawson, Walley and Williams Prizes are available for
competition for final year students at university veterinary schools in the UK
and Irish Republic. They are awarded each year by the Royal College of Veterinary Surgeons who also administer the Veterinary Drug Co (York) Ltd
Award, for students at veterinary schools in the United Kingdom who have
passed the degree course in anatomy, physiology and biochemistry. Grants
totalling up to £170 annually are available from this award for further study,
including travel study abroad, vacation courses and research study projects.

Once you have your veterinary degree and are a member of the Royal College of Veterinary Surgeons the possibilities of employment are extremely varied, and some ideas have been given at the beginning of this chapter. It may be, of course, that you will wish to go on to further study, and all six of the British universities and both Irish ones have facilities for postgraduate training. There is a long list of scholarships, fellowships and awards for postgraduate training, details of which can be obtained from the college.

But the prime subject of this book is working with horses, and this occupies the veterinary profession to an increasing extent. Up until the latter part of the last century most veterinary surgeons were employed to a very large extent with horses, but then, with the development of the internal combustion engine, horses as working animals gradually died away, and with this came a decrease in the number of vets needed to attend them. Instead farm animals — cattle, pigs and sheep — and small animals — domestic pets — filled the gap and more attention was paid to them.

After the last war, however, the horse underwent a revival, as people had more leisure time and spent more of it in riding, for pleasure, or in competition. The horse population grew to a quite staggering extent and so, automatically, the number of veterinary surgeons needed to look after them had to increase in proportion. And so it was that a dozen or so British veterinary surgeons decided that it might be useful to form the British Equine Veterinary Association, as a branch of the British Veterinary Association. An advertisement was put in a veterinary journal announcing a meeting of interested vets and a room booked for about twenty-five people. To the amazement of the organisers well over 100 turned up, and in September 1961, the BEVA was founded, with about 200 members. Now the association has nearly 800 members, of whom about 100 are from overseas, for the only other similar bodies are the American Association of Equine Practitioners and one which has just been founded in South Africa.

It was discovered that a lot of knowledge about horses and their treatment had been forgotten as a result of its lack of use, on an international as well as a national level, and the aim of the BEVA was to restore and increase this body of knowledge by a pooling of information. Not only equestrian specialists, such as those connected with racing as well as riding horses, joined the association, but many others who might be in general practice but had a particular interest in horses, and also those involved in research at the universities or at such establishments as the Equine Research Centre at Newmarket.

Each year the British Equine Veterinary Association holds a three-day congress, at which international equine specialists are invited to read papers or join in discussions.

Clearly, then, the opportunities for a veterinary surgeon who wishes to specialise in horses are considerable, both in the United Kingdom and Ireland, and overseas. And as well as in civilian life there are possibilities in the Army Veterinary and Remount Services, which a graduate would normally enter on a short service commission as lieutenant, with promotion to captain after one year's service.

It might be worth pondering what a veterinary surgeon, who does specialise in horses, remarked to me recently: 'When I became a vet I thought I would be dealing with animals, but I find at least half my time is taken up with dealing with people. Curing animals is only part of the story – it is even more important to educate the people who own them and then a lot of the troubles animals do suffer from could be avoided.'

## Animal Nursing Auxiliaries

It will be quite clear by now that the educational qualifications needed by a prospective veterinary surgeon are of a very high standard indeed, and not everyone who is looking for a career, a life even, looking after animals will be able to reach such a standard. It was for such people that the Royal College of Veterinary Surgeons introduced, in 1961, a scheme for the recruitment, training and registration of Animal Nursing Auxiliaries.

The ANA Scheme is, it should be emphasised, at present aimed at small animal nursing, but is such an important scheme that it deserves to be covered here, and could expand in the future.

Applications for trainee enrolment should be made to the RCVS, at 35 Belgrave Square, London SW1X 8QP. Requirements for enrolment are:

1    Three passes at GCE Ordinary Level or CSE Grade 1, which shall include a pass in English language and a pass in either a physical or biological science or mathematics; equivalent passes in comparable examinations in other countries will be accepted.

2    Applicant must be seventeen years of age (no upper age limit).

3    If applicant is under eighteen years of age, consent of parent or guardian is required.

4    Applicant must be gainfully employed for not less than 35 hours a week at an approved training centre (ie a veterinary practice or veterinary hospital or other veterinary centre approved under the scheme) or have the promise in writing of such employment.

Before being eligible for registration as an Animal Nursing Auxiliary, a trainee must pass two examinations. The preliminary examination may be taken at any time after trainee enrolment by the RCVS, and this examination consists of three sections:

1  A written paper on the theory and practice of nursing, Part I, with emphasis on the use of anatomy and physiology.
2  A written paper on the theory and practice of nursing, Part I, with emphasis on animal management, hygiene, nutrition, feeding, first aid, diagnostic aids and laboratory tests.
3  An oral and practical examination.

After passing the preliminary examination a trainee must wait for a further nine months, unless given special permission by the ANA Committee, before taking the final examination, which also consists of three sections:

1  A written paper on the theory and practice of nursing, Part II, medical nursing and radiography.
2  A written paper on surgical, obstetrical and paediatric nursing.
3  An oral and practical examination.

A trainee will not be eligible for registration as an ANA until completing a period of two years' training, not necessarily continuous, at an approved training centre, or centres, from the date of enrolment, and having passed both examinations.

Full-time residential courses are held at the Berkshire College of Agriculture for enrolled students who have completed at least twelve months' training at an approved centre. These courses are either of six months' (two terms') duration, from September to March, which covers the syllabus for both examinations, or of three months, from April to July, which covers the syllabus for the final examination. Attendance at such a course counts towards the required two-year period of training.

Application for entry should be made to the Principal, Berkshire College of Agriculture, Hall Place, Burchetts Green, Maidenhead, Berkshire, who will also provide full details of the courses and of grants which may be available from local education authorities.

A number of local education authorities provide part-time classes in theoretical instruction, which can supplement the practical training given at approved centres, but although the RCVS is much in favour of these and will provide a list of the courses, it does emphasise that enrolment for these courses does not, of itself, constitute enrolment as a trainee under the college's ANA Scheme.

The fees payable to the college at present are:

By trainee on application for enrolment            £5.00

By training centre (at time of application for enrolment by pro-
spective trainee)                                                    £3.00
For entry to each examination                                        £5.50
On entry to ANA register                                             £6.00

The RCVS publishes a guide to its Animal Nursing Auxiliaries Scheme
which can be obtained from the college, price 20p, which gives a great deal of
information, especially on the examinations and the syllabuses involved.

Although the college does not, itself, assist in finding employment at an approved training centre, it will provide a list of these to which prospective trainees can apply, and will also provide information about a scheme run by the
British Animal Nursing Auxiliaries Association to maintain a list of vacancies
for trainees. Careers masters may also have information about the scheme, as
will officers in the local youth employment service, who will certainly be glad
to help anyone interested in such a career.

# Farriery

Ask the majority of horsemen what they consider the one most important part of a horse and the odds are they would reply 'the foot'. The conformation may not be all that could be desired and yet the horse will still jump, race or hunt well; the head may be a bit common, the neck a little weak, a dozen things may be less than perfection without, too much, affecting the horse. But if just one of the four feet is out of action so is the whole horse; so it is small wonder that a skilled farrier, the man who makes or mars a horse's feet, is prized and much sought after. Most of you, I am sure, will know Benjamin Franklin's saying: 'For want of a nail the shoe was lost; for want of a shoe the horse was lost; for want of a horse the rider was lost.' It is as true now as it was 200 years ago when it was written.

Farriery, which in its early days included many of the functions which are now the preserve of the veterinary surgeon, is one of the oldest of occupations connected with horses. The Worshipful Company of Farriers, which received its charter from King Charles II, has been in existence for more than 600 years. Yet, even as this is being written, efforts are still being made to get a Farriers Registration Bill made law, its aim being to promote the proper shoeing of horses and training of farriers, and the prohibition of shoeing by persons unqualified to do so. When one considers the harm that can be done, and all too often is, by people shoeing horses without the proper knowledge and training, then clearly it is about time such a law was passed.

Shoeing horses is by no means necessarily the straightforward job it may appear, for it involves a great deal more than merely removing one set of shoes, preparing the hooves, and then putting on a new set. Of course in many cases, when the horse is fit and well and the feet in good condition, that is all that will be required; but horses, like people, are often less than perfectly made. It may be lame, or have a faulty action which can, in part at least, be remedied by the right sort of shoes, so that a successful farrier knows about not only the foot, but also the bones and muscles of the leg and possibly something of the make-up of the whole horse; so it was logical that for such a long time farriers were entrusted with the general welfare of the horse.

There are two apprenticeship schemes for potential farriers, both of which last for four years; one is organised and run by the Worshipful Company of Farriers, the other by the National Joint Apprenticeship Council of the National Master Farriers', Blacksmiths' and Agricultural Engineers' Association. The respective people to whom applications should be made are: Mr F. E. Birch, Registrar, Worshipful Company of Farriers, 3 Hamilton Road, Cockfosters, Barnet, Herts; and Miss R. Rowley, Registrar, NMFB & AEA, 48 Spencer Place, Leeds LS7 4BR.

Both the apprenticeship schemes are basically similar, in that they involve both practical and theoretical training. The first thing that a potential farriery apprentice needs to do is to find a master farrier willing to take him and teach him the trade (I say 'him' specifically because this is a work, often under arduous, difficult, sometimes dangerous conditions, which calls for a good deal of physical strength). This can frequently be done through the Local Small Industries Organiser, whose address can be obtained from the Youth Employment Bureau or from the Council for Small Industries in Rural Areas (CoSIRA), whose address is 35 Camp Road, Wimbledon Common, London SW19.

During the first three years of training, as well as working under, and learning from, his master, the apprentice must attend at least one course on farriery each year, under a block release scheme, at the Herefordshire Technical College or at the Royal Army Veterinary Corps Training Centre, Melton Mowbray.

The Herefordshire Technical College, whose address is Aylestone Hill, Hereford, run a number of courses, including one specifically for the Worshipful Company of Farriers; anyone who wishes to apply for an apprenticeship with the WCF should, having found a master farrier to train him, write to Mr R. Clarke, 58 Hall Park Drive, West Park, Lytham, Lancashire, for an application form. Clearly you must have your employer's permission because it will involve being away for several weeks each year. Under this

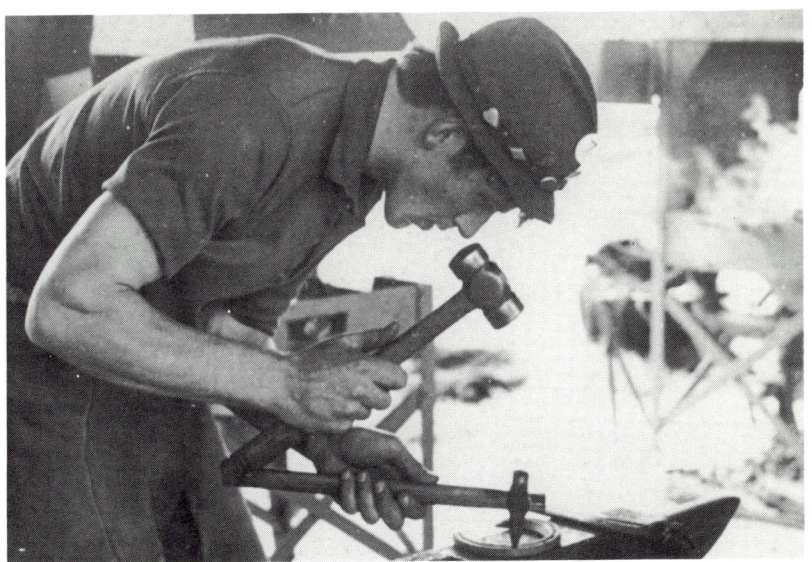

Putting the finishing touches to a horseshoe before it is fitted on to the horse. Accuracy in both making the shoe and putting it on is essential and takes years of training and practice

scheme apprentices attend the college for a five-week block of full-time farriery and smithing instruction during the first year of their apprenticeship and for a two-week period during the remaining three years of their apprenticeship. During the last attendance, apprentices sit for the Registered Shoeing Smith examination.

After a boy has served at least six months as an apprentice under this scheme the WCF may make grants to assist him with books, clothing, tools, etc. The grant, when awarded, pays £21 per month for the second six months of the first year, £15 per month for the second year, £6.50 for the third and £2.50 for the fourth.

After holding the RSS Certificate for at least two years a farrier may take the examination for Associate of the Farriery Company of London (AFCL); the highest grade of examination a farrier can take is the FWCF (Fellow of the Worshipful Company of Farriers), which can only be taken by those who have held the AFCL for not less than twelve months and who have had seven years' full-time, practical experience, including any apprenticeship period.

All three of these examinations are run by the Worshipful Company of Farriers and any farrier can take them, in order, whether or not he is an apprentice; but he must first have served at least three years as a farrier.

Boys indentured under the National Joint Apprenticeship Council Scheme do not receive direct grants but costs for attendance at the Herefordshire Technical College are invariably met by the local education authorities, from whom, in any case, permission to attend the college must be obtained. Apart from the WCF course, the Herefordshire College runs a number of others, including three four-year apprenticeship craft courses for blacksmiths and farriers. These are designed to provide three options of differing content, although there is a common element in all three sections of the course in that a wide range of craft instruction is given during the first three years of the course, and that the first attendance is for a thirteen-week block of full-time attendance which always extends from mid-September to mid-December. The courses are:

*Rural engineering course*
This is designed for general smiths' apprentices to produce a versatile type of blacksmith and general engineering craftsman.
*Industrial smiths' course*
The special emphasis of this course is on blacksmithing and fabrication craftwork.
*Farriery course*
This course, which is approved by the Worshipful Company, is designed obviously to produce a well-qualified farrier and blacksmith, complete with RSS qualifications.
During the first three years' attendance, in addition to farriery and general smithing, good practical instruction is given in gas and arc welding and bench fitting in order to produce a versatile craftsman. Optional instruction in agricultural implement repair and ornamental ironwork is available. Calculations, engineering science, including electrical safety requirements, and reading of drawings are included in the first years of the course, in addition to farriery and blacksmithing theory.

Attendance for this course involves, in the first year, thirteen weeks from mid-September to mid-December, and eight weeks in each of the three subsequent years – in the first usually from early May to early July, in the second usually from early March to early May, and in the last usually from mid-September to October.
At the end of the fourth year's attendance capable students can take the RSS examination. Apprentices indentured with the NMFB & AEA sit for Trade Tests in smithing, welding and bench fitting for their Trade Test Certificate in their final year.

The Herefordshire College also runs two other farriery courses. For those who already hold the RSS Certificate and wish to obtain the AFCL there is a course consisting of a fortnight's full-time attendance in which both the practical and theoretical work required is covered. Intending students must apply to the Registrar of the Worshipful Company for permission to take the examination several weeks before they attend the course. Two AFCL courses are held at Hereford each year, the first usually starting in early March and the second in mid-March.

Both the AFCL and RSS examinations are held twice a year – on the third Wednesday in March and October – at selected centres approved by the WCF, of which the Herefordshire College is one.

The college also runs a course for adult blacksmith/farriers who wish to pass the RSS examination. This is a six-week block release course. Intending students must comply with the WCF's required conditions of practical experience and must apply to the Registrar of the company for permission to sit the examination. The course is usually run from late January to early March. The RSS examination consists of practical work of shoe making and horse shoeing together with a combined oral and written test.

CoSIRA also give training in farriery; for some eighteen years this was by means of consultant farriers, but such has been the demand that they have decided to re-appoint a farriery office. Their Advisory Services Division, as well as publishing a number of books, including *Farriery – Some Questions and Answers* and *The Horse's Foot*, may well be able to help if you have any particular problems.

There are a number of other books which could be both interesting and useful, but as these in some cases overlap with other subjects covered they are listed in the bibliography at the back.

Horace Hayes's excellent work *Veterinary Notes for Horse Owners*, originally published in 1877 but reprinted and revised many times since then, contains a particularly absorbing chapter on shoeing, including the necessity of doing it at all, and emphasising the 'false economy' of neglecting this. The hoof takes from eight to twelve months, or sometimes slightly longer, to grow from top to bottom and should be attended to at least every four weeks.

There are two types of shoeing – hot and cold. Hot shoeing is very much to be preferred, because the shoes can then be made exactly to the horse's requirements. The disadvantages of the factory-made shoes are that because they are mass-produced they will not exactly fit the hoof; also, because the nail holes will always be in the same places, parts of the hoof are over-used. A farrier who makes his own shoes buys the iron in bars and makes up the shoes exactly as needed.

To start with, of course, the old shoes have to be removed and the feet prepared, ie the hoof trimmed and ragged parts of the sole and frog removed, a most delicate operation. Then the hot shoe is held against the foot to test for accuracy or to see what alterations need to be made. The problem is that, for hot shoeing, a fire and anvil are necessary and they are not always available. A farrier shoeing certain horses regularly may sometimes make sets of shoes at his own forge and then take them to the horse.

There are a number of different types of shoe, varying in shape and the material used according to the horse being shod; if the horse is doing a lot of road work they will be simpler and stronger than for, say, a hunter; and again a racehorse, with his lightweight 'plates', is a different proposition altogether. Working with racehorses is especially delicate work; imagine 'pricking' the favourite just before he is about to run in the Derby! A farrier who works with racehorses frequently specialises, sometimes completely, in such animals if for no other reason than that, having gained the confidence of a number of trainers in a particular area, he is too much in demand to have time for any but racehorses. The Levy Board, keen to encourage youngsters into a vital part of racing, subsidise apprentices' wages, and it is as well to remember that in your early years as a farriery apprentice you will certainly not be earning a fortune; the National Joint Wages Board for the Farriery, Blacksmith and Agricultural Engineering Trade have agreed rates, payable to apprentices in proportion to the full rate, which are 35 per cent in the first year, 50 per cent in the second, 75 per cent in the third and 90 per cent in the fourth. This is written into an agreement when a boy is apprenticed under the Worshipful Company of Farriers' scheme.

As well as the straightforward functional shoes for a sound horse in work, there are a variety of shoes, or adaptations, that can be used for surgical purposes: for prevention of brushing; for reducing a tendency to over-reach or under-reach; for horses with tendon injuries or laminitis; and a great deal more.

The mythical blacksmith, huge and bronzed, merrily swinging his hammer under the village chestnut tree is, like most such romantic visions, so much an exception as to be almost, if not quite, an illusion. Farriers do the bulk of their work indoors over a hot forge, and although strength is important it is only one factor in a craft which calls for skill, patience and ingenuity.

If, or when, the Farriers Registration Bill becomes law, training or proven experience will be a necessary qualification for anyone who wishes to shoe horses other than his own. But even if it is not needed by law it is clearly advisable. Farriery is not a career anyone would be likely to drift into for the money that can be earned, and if you want to become a farrier for the satisfaction that you can get from the job then clearly you will want to be as accomplished as possible. Although it may often be a hard job, it is one which, if you are a gregarious person, will enable you to get out and meet a lot of people as well as a lot of horses. In due course you will probably be your own master, doing a vitally important job and one which, in as much as anything can be guaranteed in these changing times, looks certain to offer a lot of opportunities for a long time to come.

# Bloodstock and Transport Agencies

## Bloodstock Agencies

A great many people come into racing knowing little more about the sport than that they enjoy it; they like the thrill of going racing and want to get more closely involved by owning a horse of their own. And just as, if you are buying or selling a house or a car you will probably do it through any agent, so with buying, and perhaps eventually selling, a horse. There are about a dozen bloodstock agencies in Britain and probably the total number of people employed on a permanent basis is no more than 300–400 so that clearly, for those who are interested in the work, there is a great deal of competition for the available places. There is a great deal of variety in the work of a big bloodstock agency, and as a pattern one might take the biggest of all in this country, the British Bloodstock Agency, whose main base is in London but who also have offices and a house at Newmarket – 'headquarters' of British racing – and a stud at Enfield, a sort of transit camp for horses.

Selling is the major work of the agency, but the department dealing with stallion nominations and shares is not far behind it – a few years ago it earned the agency as much as the selling side, but since then, because of the economic situation, fewer horses have been syndicated at stud and this has dropped away a little. And then there are the various ancillary departments: insurance, which is vital when dealing with bloodstock which can be worth many thousands of pounds; shipping; valuing; pedigrees; and also the stud at Enfield.

The buying and selling side is the one which most people find attractive, especially those wanting to 'break into' the business, and it really is big business; for example, at the 1974 Newmarket December sales, which are the year's biggest sales of bloodstock in Britain and last about a week, the BBA spent well over £1 million buying horses on behalf of their clients, around a quarter of the total sales.

The Australian poet 'Banjo' Patterson wrote a few lines which every bloodstock agent might well have pinned over his bed.

> We want you to buy us a horse,
> It must have the speed to catch swallows,
> And stamina with it, of course;
> The price ain't a thing that'll grieve us,
> It's getting a bad 'un annoys.

Time and again one hears or reads of horses that were bought for a pittance winning a major race; and against that, of horses which were bought as foals or yearlings for large sums of money and are now about to make a first appearance over hurdles having failed dismally to make any sort of mark on the flat or to repay more than a fraction of the purchase price. To those who know the racing game this is all part of it; apart from actually breeding a champion there can be nothing more satisfying than spotting one before anyone else does. But this takes time and experience with, for the occasional fortunate being, that 'eye' for a horse in its rawest state which is the nearest possible equivalent to a crystal ball.

Asked for his opinion on the necessary qualities for a bloodstock agent, Colonel Robin Hastings, the senior director of the British Bloodstock Agency, replied:

A knowledge of racing, and that is something hard to define, but either you know about it or you don't; he must know people in racing; he must know about studs and breeding; he must go down well with people. And he must be honest. It is no good thinking you can walk about a racecourse with a cigar in your mouth and just be a bloodstock agent – it is hard work.

So what advice would he give to someone about to leave school or university who wanted to go into the bloodstock agency business?

I'd tell him to go away and learn, for a long time. First, go to a trainer, spend a year with him at least. And then at least one season at a good stud, under a man who would really teach him. Then he should go round the world, to Australia and South America, working in studs and training stables. It's possible to get temporary work in the United States – one of our clients each year has two, three or four Englishmen to help with his yearlings. But even then, if someone came back to Britain after doing all that I could not guarantee him a job. We have a comparatively small staff and they mostly tend to stay. We don't sack anybody so there is not much opportunity.

For example, our youngest executive, if you like, who is twenty-eight, did all that I have recommended; he failed as a vet, but knows something about it, and was trying to work for us for years. Each December he would go to the sales and help with our horses. Finally he won his place and we have just sent him for six months to America.

As in any sort of job where the demand so far exceeds the supply, to get the employment you want takes knowledge, application, persistence – and a touch of luck. The BBA's total staff only numbers about thirty-five and many of the other agencies would be a good deal less than that. Most of the other jobs in the agency involve a lot of book and paper work, but allied to a knowledge of horses and racing. Especially is this true of the stallion department, whose head has a great deal of influence. He must be able to say what stallions are available, and whether they are likely to be suitable to the mare in question; where the proposed stallion stands, and what is his fertility. He must have a good eye to the market.

He will be helped by the pedigree department in all this, especially with the suitability of the bloodlines of a particular mare and stallion. This is a fascinating but highly complex study, which has become more so with the increased internationalisation of the sport, with stallions from the United States coming to stand in England, France or Ireland as well as the interchange of horses throughout Europe and an increasing inflow from the southern hemisphere – Australia and New Zealand. Trying to evaluate the comparative worth, from a breeding viewpoint, of horses from such a wide area inevitably calls for a knowledge of, and interest in, racing in all parts of the world.

The average number of stallions managed by the BBA is around thirty to forty, mostly in this country with one or two in Ireland, although most that stand in that country are passed on to the fairly autonomous subsidiary, BBA (Ireland).

Inevitably with the increased value of bloodstock the insurance side has become more important and complex. Not so long ago all that was needed was a knowledge of horses and of how the agency itself worked, but not now; the present head of the department had years of experience at Lloyd's. Clearly with such a small staff, training facilities are limited to the point of being almost non-existent, so that experience has to have been gained beforehand. As with the insurance, so with the shipping, whose present head had eighteen years with P&O, while two others were both previously with Lep, one of the country's leading transport agencies.

The stud at Enfield is run in very much a father-to-son tradition, although there is very often a vacancy for a groom there, with the possibility of travel thrown in. Usually there are about seven or eight grooms employed at the stud.

It will be clear by now that bloodstock agency work is not something you can go into straight away; experience is vital, knowledge of racing and breeding and, because you are dealing with people both as prospective clients and as possible sellers of horses, you must know racing people on a wide scale. But if you do break into it, it is absorbing work, and rewarding too.

## Transport Agencies

The increased international aspect of racing has had a considerable effect on the business of transporting horses, but racehorses are only a part of their scheme of operations. Polo ponies, show jumpers, eventers, trotters, all help to make up the payloads, and create their own particular problems. Problems which have multiplied with the increase in bureaucracy and its attendant red-tape throughout the world, and which have been made more immediate by the increasing use of air transport rather than sea and land. As a result, agencies have built up dealing exclusively with the business of getting horses from one part of the globe to another, of which the two biggest in this country are Lep and Pedens.

Pedens, to take them as an example of how such an agency works, divide their transport up basically into three major sections, starting with the short-haul business of racehorses and other bloodstock – broodmares and foals – between Britain, Ireland and most of the continental countries where racing is popular – France, Germany, Italy, Belgium, Norway and so on. Of this ninety-nine per cent is by air, the racehorses travelling with their own grooms, with someone going along who has experience of flying, while most of the broodmares are accompanied by Pedens grooms.

The majority of grooms who work for Pedens do so on a freelance basis and they need, for the flying, more experience than merely having worked with horses. They must be quiet but firm, able to calm an excited thoroughbred perhaps flying for the first time and inclined to panic and must have sufficient knowledge to be able to judge how far to rely upon their own powers of persuasion and when it may be necessary to dope a horse – a last resort but sometimes a very necessary one. Says Paul Penfold, a director of Pedens: 'A horse, if

Leading a horse quietly into his horsebox and making sure he is happily settled is important if the journey is not to upset him

it is going to be doped, must be doped *before* it goes beserk. Otherwise it will be too late. Flying horses is not like taking them by road – if a horse panics in a box you can quickly stop and let him out, but obviously you cannot do that in an aeroplane.'

There is a great deal of traffic with Australia and New Zealand, the vast majority of which used to be by sea. But Australia has very strict quarantine regulations, and after the outbreak a few years ago of Venezuelan equine encephalitis in the Panama Canal area they refused to admit horses that had travelled through the canal, which made the journey much longer. So Pedens designed special boxes – padded and air-conditioned – which could be loaded on to aircraft. Horses are accepted into Australia after a two-week quarantine period in England and now Pedens have a chartered Boeing 707 with twenty-nine horses on board flying to Australia and New Zealand every three or four weeks; the journey takes about 28–30hrs, compared with a month on a boat. This is not necessarily an arduous journey for a horse, and Pedens were very proud of a broodmare, with her foal, that they recently sent to Australia who, immediately on landing, was boxed 800 miles to a major show and won the broodmare championship.

On the return part of these regular trips the 707 will often pick up trotters in Australia, fly them to New York, unload them there, collect some broodmares and foals, and fly these back to Europe.

The Argentine is Europe's main source of polo ponies so there is a big movement of these, some by boat but most by air. There is also a tremendous trade with the United States; twice weekly 707s fly with a full load of twenty-nine horses to America and return with twenty-nine.

There is also the business of transporting the competition horses – the show jumpers – to shows all over Europe and North America, and also of transporting the horses sold to go abroad or bought to return to England. It all adds up to a lot of horses, and in 1974 Pedens alone handled well over 4,000.

The paper-work involved is prodigious, and the twenty or so permanent staff employed have their hands full; for instance a horse has to have a different veterinary certificate for each country it passes through, so a show jumper going to compete in Lisbon, for example, would have to have certificates for France, Spain and Portugal, as well as an extraordinary number of papers for various government departments – customs, ministries of agriculture etc. As an example of their proliferation, in 1970 just two customs forms were needed – one for a horse going into a country and one for coming out – at the latest count there were twelve forms needed. The problems can be increased by human error, such as when a horsebox driver goes to the wrong frontier post instead of the one where a veterinary official, who must check the horses and sign the papers, is waiting; or by natural causes, such as when a too-rough Channel prevents horses sailing at all.

So the people who attend to the paper-work need to have a fair knowledge of horses and the sort of things that can happen to them to prevent inconvenient and costly mistakes. Such as happened not long ago with Pedens.

Pilar Munro-Wilson, who as Pilar Cepeda rode for Peru in the 1970 World Show Jumping Championship and then settled in England and married an Englishman, brought two Peruvian horses with her to Belgium and then asked Pedens to bring them over from Belgium to England. For one reason or another the horsebox bringing them was late getting to the port of embarkation in Belgium and hurriedly drove on to the boat without having the papers checked by the customs; so a little while later Pedens were presented with a bill from the Belgian Government for £3,000 for horses which, although physically in England, were, according to their records, still in Belgium, and as the time in which they were in bond had expired their value was now due. After some two years of 'negotiation' Pedens finally had to pay £1,500 merely because one of their employees had not had his papers stamped.

Which is just an example of the need for absolute accuracy and working 'to the book'; but given an interest in horses and the right sort of training it might well be a job worth thinking about.

# On The Fringe

The vast majority of jobs and careers working with or near horses have been covered in the foregoing chapters, but there are a variety of others which may make some sort of appeal to horse-lovers; work in which perhaps the horses, although important to you as a person, may be called incidental. Or jobs which are so limited in number that your chance of making a living out of them would seem to be remote – yet some people do so and a few hints on how to go about it may be useful.

## Police

All over Britain horses are used by the police, and although only a small section of the total police force, the mounted branches have a vitally important part to play. As a means of controlling a crowd which has got out of hand, or is in danger of doing so, or is merely so big that men on foot are physically unable to make their presence felt, horses are ideal. The horse is basically a very gentle and careful animal; see a horse or rider fall in a race and you will notice how, if it is at all possible, the other horses will try to avoid treading on them. So it is that a mounted policeman can use his horse to push back a crowd, or prevent one breaking through a cordon, without causing any harm to that crowd. Of course there may occasionally be a trodden toe, but the calmness of a police horse, often under the most extreme pressure, is something to wonder at and a tribute to their training.

One of the most famous of police horse training establishments in the world is at Imber Court, East Molesey, Surrey, which caters not only for the Metropolitan and City of London Police, but for a number from the provinces and even from overseas. The establishment was founded in 1920 by Colonel Laurie, and the horses trained there have played an important part in some of the historic events of Britain's capital city, as indeed they have since horses were first introduced into London law-enforcement in the eighteenth century.

Originally the police tended to use heavy, rather common, horses but Colonel Laurie introduced a much better-bred strain, thoroughbreds some of them and even an occasional ex-racehorse. It is a particular credit to the training that these horses receive at Imber Court that, after all the excitements of a racing career, they can be brought to a state of sufficient calmness to be usable for police duties. They are trained by a permanent staff before being allotted to a particular police officer for duty. These officers are then, until they reach the rank of inspector, responsible for looking after their own horses.

Each year police horses from all over the country journey to the Horse of the Year Show at the Empire Pool, Wembley, to contest the title of 'Police Horse of the Year', and the tests they have to go through – crashing and discordant noises, flapping flags or whatever waved inches from their faces, and so on – are ample proof of their training. There is a growing tendency for police officers to take part in equestrian competition, horse trials and show jumping, and one of the most consistent of competitors, Police Constable Bob Hurford of the Metropolitan Police, riding Sandown, has also a remarkable record at Wembley: in 1974 they won the Police Horse of the Year title for the third time.

As well as crowd control, police horses are used for escort duties, including royal processions, and also, in some parts of the country, for patrolling terrain which could otherwise only be covered on foot. If you are interested in police work your local police station would be able to tell you the address to write to for particulars in your area. To take the Thames Valley Police as an example, it is possible to become a police cadet at sixteen, or seventeen for girls, for preliminary training before joining the force at nineteen. If you have four 'O' Levels or the equivalent in CSE (Grade 1), including mathematics and English language, you may be exempted from the entrance examination. Good health is, naturally, essential, and certain height qualifications must be fulfilled.

Somewhat akin to police work are the mounted keepers who patrol certain parks, such as the Royal Parks near London, at Richmond and Bushey Park, Hampton Court. This work, which comes under the jurisdiction of the Department of the Environment, is pleasant, in attractive surroundings, but employs only a handful of men.

Although the army has become largely mechanised, horses are still used for certain ceremonial duties, and the Royal Army Veterinary Corps establishment at Melton Mowbray, Leicestershire, is a well-equipped centre for the study of animal health. A local recruiting office would be able to give details.

## Circus

There was a time when travelling circuses came, sooner or later, to just about every town in the land, and a good many villages too; staying for a few days, then down would come the Big Top, and they would be on their way again. The taste in entertainment is not what it was and circuses are much fewer now, but the life in them can still be interesting and exciting, and is certainly varied. Men tend to be employed in circuses, although one of the best known of animal trainers in Britain today is Mary Chipperfield.

Work in a circus has a particular interest for horse-lovers, not only because the Liberty Horses are among the most enjoyed of the acts but because it is possible to work with horses that are being trained from a comparatively 'green' condition up to quite advanced high-school movements.

There is no formalised training, and at the start it would be a case of working as a groom, watching and learning techniques. Because a circus is show business, presentation is all-important, so that you will have to learn to produce horses in their best possible condition, well-trained and obedient but still gay and with flair. Horses tend to like a routine, and because a circus is constantly moving this becomes even more important than for horses who return each night to their own familiar surroundings.

Because circus people are so used to travelling, because it is an integral part of their way of life, it is by no means too uncomfortable. Occasionally you might need to rough it, but that is perhaps a small price to pay for the chance of working with well-trained horses, in glamorous surroundings, and of travelling widely both in Britain and abroad.

## Outside the Ring

We have dealt with the possibilities of a career in the ring, showing, show jumping and so on, but there are a lot of people outside the ring who contribute towards the success of a show or competition. Many of these people, judges, timing officials for the jumping events, and stewards, may be working in a purely honorary capacity; perhaps it is their local county or village show and they are happy to play their part without expecting any financial reward for it. These days most shows are so hard-pressed that without a good deal of

Mrs Pamela Carruthers, course-builder at many international shows all over the world, checking a fence at the famous Hickstead, Sussex, showground

voluntary labour they would be unable to survive; indeed many shows have faded from the calendar simply because of lack of support. But most of the bigger shows also have a nucleus of permanent paid staff. Running a county show, for example, is a full-time job, and virtually the moment one year's show is over plans are being made for the next year.

Usually this permanent staff is fairly small: a secretary, possibly working under an honorary committee, who is assisted by just a handful of girls. The snag about this sort of job is that when the horses are actually there on the showground the people running the show are likely to be at their busiest with hardly a moment to stand and stare. The qualifications needed for such a job are basically similar to those needed for any office work. The two London shows, the Royal International and the Horse of the Year Show, have a permanent office in London, and originally the offices of the British Horse Society and the British Show Jumping Association were in London too, but now they are located at the National Equestrian Centre on the royal showground at Kenilworth, near Leamington Spa in Warwickshire.

Not only the BHS and the BSJA have their headquarters there, but also the Pony Club, the Combined Training and Dressage Groups; it has become the hub of much of the horse activity of the country, is growing in size, and offers quite a possibility of an 'office job' with a difference, situated as it is in the country. Quite a number of the people who work there are able to keep their own horses nearby, which one could hardly do working in a big city.

It has been said that the most important man in a show jumping competition is the course-builder, and certainly he can make or mar a competition no matter how good the horses and riders taking part may be. To be able to judge the quality of the entry for a particular competition and then build a course to suit it – one that is not so difficult that there will be no clear rounds, nor yet so easy that there will be too many; a course which encourages the horses to jump boldly but gives the rider something to think about; one which is attractive for the spectators to watch – is something of an art.

As with so many jobs connected with horses there is no formalised training, and the majority of course-builders seem to have 'drifted' into it; many have had some experience of riding in show jumping competitions themselves, but not necessarily. The late John Gross, tragically killed while driving from one show to another, had hardly ever ridden let alone show jumped, but he worked closely with Colonel Jack Talbot-Ponsonby, a triple winner of the King George V Gold Cup and then for many years course-builder at the London shows, and as a result became an accomplished course-builder in his own right.

Working with an established course-builder is clearly the only real way to start, and it will be a long time before you can expect to do it on a professional basis. When you are recognised, however, the possibilities are considerable; for example, both Pamela Carruthers, the resident course-builder at the All-England Jumping Course at Hickstead, and Alan Ball, the BSJA's official course-builder, are regularly invited to build courses at some of the big overseas shows. Although there is no particular training for course-building, its importance has been recognised by the foundation in 1974 of the Embassy Trophy for course-building, to be decided by a committee of experts including Mrs Carruthers.

Course-builders also play a big part in horse trials, and have the additional responsibility of not hurting the horses competing over their cross-country fences. The British Horse Society has a number of official horse trials course-builders, of whom the doyen is Bill Thomson, a qualified veterinary surgeon who builds the courses for the three-day event at Burghley, which has twice staged the world championship, and at many other smaller trials throughout the country. Frank Weldon who is both the director of the Badminton event and the course-builder there was himself an Olympic team gold medal winner.

## Saddlery

Strictly speaking saddlery does not qualify as 'working with horses', for only rarely would a saddler actually be working with a horse, for example when making a saddle to measure. But clearly without the saddler's products those who do spend their whole lives with horses would, to say the least, be hard put to carry on their work.

Saddlery, in which generic term one includes bridle-making and all other tack, is a rewarding occupation which has directly benefited from the considerable increase in horses and riding over the past few years, and there has been a parallel increase in demand for saddlers, either to make saddles and bridles from scratch or to repair them. In the old days anyone who wanted to become a saddler, and very often it would be a family business passed on from father to son, would learn the craft from someone already established; this is still done to a large extent, but there are courses in saddlery which a boy, or girl, can take on leaving school, and courses also for those who, already working with a saddler, wish to increase their skill.

It scarcely needs emphasising that anyone contemplating a career with horses, for example with the intention of eventually running a riding school, would benefit considerably from such a course; not only from vastly increased knowledge of the tack involved, but also from being able to do your own repairs to saddlery, which can be a considerable item of expense.

With little doubt the most satisfactory way to become a saddler is to take the rural saddlery course which is run each year by the Cordwainers Technical College at Hackney in London. Until 1975 this was a two-part course, beginning in September of each year; the first 'in college' period was of twenty-seven weeks' duration, and the second, after two years of workshop practice, was a short, intensive college course of approximately six weeks' duration.

In 1975, however, a straight nine-month course was introduced, giving a very thorough basic training not only in the making of saddles and bridles but also in all the other aspects of running a saddlery business: costings, bookkeeping, materials science, riding boot repairs, machining and liberal studies. The object of the course is 'to widen the practical ability and improve the skill and technical knowledge of the saddlery apprentice, or of those concerned with horses or riding'.

The entry requirements for the course are:

Aged sixteen or over.
Be a trainee or apprentice for saddlery.
Be engaged in the trade or allied trade, with a wish to improve technical knowledge and ability.

The qualifications for which students are prepared are the City and Guilds of London Certificates in Rural Saddlery, Parts I and II, and the syllabus covers all aspects of technological and practical work which the rural saddler is likely to meet.

The fee for the course in 1975 was £75, but students may be eligible for an award from their local education authority, to whom, in any case, if they live outside the area of the Inner London Education Authority, they have to apply for permission to attend a course at the Cordwainers College. Students under eighteen years on 1 September of the year they take the course are also invited by the college to apply for one of a number of bursaries awarded by the Worshipful Company of Cordwainers and the Worshipful Company of Curriers, which are valued at approximately £75 annually.

Any youngster interested in a career in saddlery and in attending the course should write to the Secretary, Cordwainers Technical College, Mare Street, Hackney, London E8 3RE.

CoSIRA (mentioned in the chapter on farriery) is also concerned with instruction in saddlery. Formerly called the Rural Industries Bureau, it is as much an advisory body as a teaching one, but it does have a department which gives courses and also instructors who travel the country giving training and tuition in saddlers' own establishments. It also published, in 1973, a textbook called *Making A Saddle* which would be of considerable use and interest to anyone contemplating a career in saddlery. The council's address is PO Box 717, 35 Camp Road, Wimbledon Common, London SW19 4UP.

CoSIRA run a series of four courses each year at their training centre for saddlers, journeymen and apprentices in their second and third year. These are a five-day course covering the principles and practices of saddle-making; a five-day course in harness-making to help saddlers, apprentices and others who have been out of touch with harness work to respond to the renewed interest in driving; a three-day course in making and repairing bellows; and a five-day course for the semi-proficient who wish to improve their skills and knowledge.

It may well be that you hope, eventually, to start your own business as a saddler, and in this CoSIRA will be able to assist you in a number of ways; with advice on business management, for example, or financial loans for workshop, working capital and equipment. The council can also help to publicise small businesses through its 'Guide to Country Workshops in Britain', which lists, county by county, workshops and retail craft shops, with descriptions of the sort of work carried out.

There are still fewer really well-trained and competent saddlers than are needed throughout the country, and if working with leather, and indirectly with horses, appeals to you, you can be virtually assured of a satisfying job once you have completed your basic training.

## Photography

It is possible for anyone wanting to become a professional photographer to take a course of training, and although the majority of those likely to be seen around the ringside at a show jumping competition, or tucked away by a cross-country fence during a horse trial, may not have actually taken such a course there are obvious advantages in having as great a knowledge as possible of the instrument that, hopefully, is going to help you make a living. A number of technical colleges and colleges of art have courses, lasting two or three years, leading to the intermediate and final examinations of the Institute of British Photographers. A fairly high level of general education is required to be able to take these courses and details will probably be available from your local education authority.

With these qualifications there are clearly a number of jobs open to you, and it must be said that photographing horses exclusively is not likely to be among the most lucrative although, if you have a particular interest in them, it can clearly be very satisfying. Photographing horses, indeed any animal, calls for particular skills apart from the technical ones with the camera; standing still, a horse may look either graceful or positively ungainly according to his stance, and the ability to 'stand' a horse is an invaluable asset to a horse photographer which is only acquired after a good deal of experience.

Photographing horses in action, be they show jumpers, trials horses or race-horses, hackneys or show horses, calls for a quick eye, almost an intuitive one so that you get to know how a horse is going to look a fraction of a second before he actually does. Leslie Lane, one of the foremost of British horse photo-graphers, wrote an article in the 1974 edition of the *Horse and Rider Yearbook* which, although mainly intended for amateurs wishing to photograph for fun, nevertheless has some advice that could be useful to anyone.

If you intend to live by your camera, taking photographs is only one side of the business. The other is to sell them. Some photographers concentrate on sel-ling the photographs to the people in them, and it is perhaps a tribute to man's vanity that so many of us like nothing better than to see a picture of ourselves riding well over a jump or round the ring. The majority sell for publication, either in the specialist magazines or in books or newspapers – usually all three. There are not that many horse magazines, and newspapers very often prefer to send their own staff photographers to an important event, although they will take others' pictures for 'stock', to be put in the picture library until they are needed. It is quite possible to sell photographs abroad as well, and many find this a rather more lucrative business than confining their activities to British publications, but it is a very individual business which needs to be built up over the years.

The equipment, not only cameras, spare lenses and developing gear, but also the 'consumer goods', film, chemicals and so on, are expensive and getting more so, which makes setting up as a freelance a costly business. It might be best to start working for a general photographic agency, taking time off for your own speciality until such time as you can stand on your own feet.

## Journalism

If this looks a case of 'leaving the best till last', I can only say that I have been accused, and I use the word advisedly, more than once of having 'the best job in Fleet Street'; and although that is partly a case of the other man's grass looking greener it would be hypocritical to pretend that it is other than a highly enjoy-able way of earning a living – as any man who is paid for doing what he enjoys doing anyway must find.

As with photography, there are many ways into horse-journalism, and most of them have rather more to do with horses than with journalism. For example, my predecessor on the *Daily Telegraph*, the late Captain Lionel Dawson, had a distinguished career in the Royal Navy before he joined the paper as hunting correspondent and then, with the changes in fashion, wrote less and less about hunting and increasingly more about shows, in particular the hunter classes. Although it would be true to say he was employed originally for his knowledge of horses and hunting, this did not stop him writing extremely well, pungently and to the point, which alas is something a great many people who know a great deal about horses are unable to do.

Therefore, although horses may be your great interest, there is everything to be said in favour of professional training. There are now training schemes but these are complementary, rather than alternative, to working for a newspaper. A reasonably high standard of education is clearly essential and a university degree can be an advantage, although there are those who avow that it is better to start on a newspaper as early as possible. Whenever you start it will have to be at the bottom as a trainee, probably on a weekly or local paper, and if you tell the editor then that you want to specialise in horses you could be in for a rude answer. When you are permitted to go out reporting you will have to cover every mundane thing you are instructed to, from baby shows to parish council meetings.

Only when you get to provincial daily paper level are you even likely to be able to specialise in sports generally, and of these horses are likely to take a fairly unimportant place behind the local football, cricket and rugby teams. But horse shows and point-to-points are of growing public interest and, as a general rule, newspapers report what the public is interested in.

If your hope is to join a national newspaper and travel round the shows, both at home and overseas, or write about racing, then, if it is not too immodest to say so, your knowledge of your subject and your range of contacts, which are the life-blood of any newspaperman, must be fairly extensive. There is nothing more certain to bring in a flood of letters – mostly vituperous and the majority suggesting that the writer of the letter should take over the newspaper job – than the slightest error of fact or deviation from accepted opinion.

This is probably the main reason that writers on horses have tended to be recruited from outside the newspaper industry, presumably on the theory that, as long as their facts are right, their verbosity can be dealt with by an experienced sub-editor in the office. In this equestrian journalism differs from almost every other type of sports writing, and must have something to do with the mystique that non-horsey people ascribe to the horse.

Newspapers are few in number and decreasing, it seems, almost hourly, but the specialist magazines offer an alternative source of employment, although their permanent staffs are, for economic reasons, fairly small. The majority of them tend to rely for the bulk of their contributions on outsiders who work on a freelance basis. If you are employed on a local paper it may well be possible to contribute in this way, which will both supplement your income and give you an entrée to the sort of work you are seeking and, incidentally, increase your range of contacts.

Writing is something which, because of its essentially precarious nature, one would hesitate to recommend as a way of earning a living, but those who feel drawn to it will probably not be put off by any doubts, and if they are they are probably wise to be so. Suffice it to say that it has taken me to a lot of places I should probably not otherwise have visited and introduced me to many people I should not otherwise have known; and that, for me, is enough.

# Useful Addresses

Association of British Riding Schools
   Chesham House, 56 Green End Road, Sawtry, Huntingdon PE17 5OY.
British Horse Society
   National Equestrian Centre, Kenilworth, Warwickshire CV8 2LR.
British Show Hack & Cob Association
   *as* British Horse Society.
British Show Jumping Association
   *as* British Horse Society.
British Veterinary Association
   7 Mansfield Street, Portland Place, London W1.
Cordwainers Technical College
   Mare Street, Hackney, London E8 3RE.
Council for Small Industries in Rural Areas (CoSIRA)
   35 Camp Road, Wimbledon Common, London SW19.
Herefordshire Technical College
   Aylestone Hill, Hereford.
Horserace Betting Levy Board
   17/23 Southampton Row, London WC2.
Hunters Improvement Society
   National Westminster Bank Chambers, 8 Market Square, Westerham, Kent.
Hurlingham Polo Association
   60 Mark Lane, London, EC3R 7TJ.

Masters of Foxhounds Association
  The Elm, Chipping Norton, Oxon.
National Master Farriers', Blacksmiths' and Agricultural Engineers' Association
  48 Spencer Place, Leeds, Yorkshire.
National Pony Society
  Stoke Lodge, 85 Cliddesden Road, Basingstoke, Hants.
Pony Club
  *as* British Horse Society.
Racing Information Bureau
  42 Portman Square, London W1.
Royal College of Veterinary Surgeons
  32 Belgrave Square, London SW1.
Society of Master Saddlers
  9 St Thomas Street, London SE1.
Thoroughbred Breeders Association
  42 Portman Square, London W1.
Weatherby & Sons
  41 Portman Square, London W1.
Worshipful Company of Farriers
  3 Hamilton Road, Cockfosters, Barnet, Herts EH4 9EU.
Worshipful Company of Saddlers
  Gutter Lane, London EC4.

# Select Bibliography

Becker, F. *The Breed of the Racehorse*, British Bloodstock Agency, 1935
British Horse Society. *Manual of Horsemanship*, 1950 (reprint 1967)
Campbell, Judith. *Police Horses*, David & Charles (Newton Abbot), 1967
CoSIRA. *Making a Saddle*, 1973
Edwards, E. *Saddlery*, J. A. Allen, 1963
Hayes, M. *Veterinary Notes for Horse Owners*, Stanley Paul, 1877 (many revisions, latest 1968)
Herbert, Ivor. *Winter's Tale*, Pelham, 1974
Hislop, John. *Steeplechasing*, Hutchinson, 1951
———. *The Brigadier*, Secker & Warburg, 1973
Kellock, E. M. *The Story of Riding*, David & Charles (Newton Abbot), 1974
Larter, Chris. *Around the World – for a Horse*, A. H. & A. W. Reed (Wellington, NZ), 1970
Ligertwood, Kenneth. *Huntsmen of Our Time*, Pelham, 1968
Lonsdale Library. *Foxhunting*, Seeley, Service & Co, 1930
———. *Polo*, Seeley, Service & Co, 1936
Martin, Ann. *The Trainers*, Stanley Paul, 1972
Miller, Prof William. *Practical Essentials in the Care and Management of Horses on Thoroughbred Studs*, Thoroughbred Breeding Association, 1965
Podhajsky, Alois. *The Complete Training of Horse and Rider*, Harrap, 1967
———. *The Riding Teacher*, Harrap, 1973
Pony Club. *A Guide to Pony Trekking*, 1973
Rodzianko, Paul. *Modern Horsemanship*, Seeley, Service & Co, 1936
Sharpe, Harry. *The Practical Stud Groom*, British Bloodstock Agency, 1930

# Acknowledgements

Many people have helped me in the preparation of this book, and I should particularly like to thank Mr S. M. Algar, Industrial Training Officer of CoSIRA; Mr F. E. Birch, Registrar of the Worshipful Company of Farriers; Mrs Jenny Botsford, Press Secretary, British Veterinary Association; Mr Raymond Brooks-Ward; Mr J. A. Cunningham, PRO, British Equine Veterinary Association; Mr Findlay Davidson; Mr A. M. Huline Dickens, Saddlery Lecturer, Cordwainers Technical College; Brigadier J. R. C. Gannon, Secretary, Hurlingham Polo Association; Mr Johnnie Gilbert; Miss Louise Gold, Assistant Director, Racing Information Bureau; Lieutenant Colonel C. R. D. Gray, Director, The National Stud; Colonel N. Grove-White, Development Officer, British Horse Society; Lieutenant Colonel Robin Hastings, Director, British Bloodstock Agency; Mr G. W. Kemp, Vice Principal, Herefordshire Technical College; Mr Peter Kingdom, Saddlery Officer, CoSIRA; Mr Leslie Lane; Mrs Joan I. Plumb, Secretary to the Education Committee, Royal College of Veterinary Surgeons; Major General J. R. Reynolds, Director General, British Horse Society; Miss R. Rowley, General Secretary, National Master Farriers', Blacksmiths' and Agricultural Engineers' Association; and Mr S. G. Sheppard, Secretary, Thoroughbred Breeders' Association.

# Index